SPORTS ENCYCLOPEDIAS

THE NHL ENCYCLOPEDIA

BY DAVID J. CLARKE

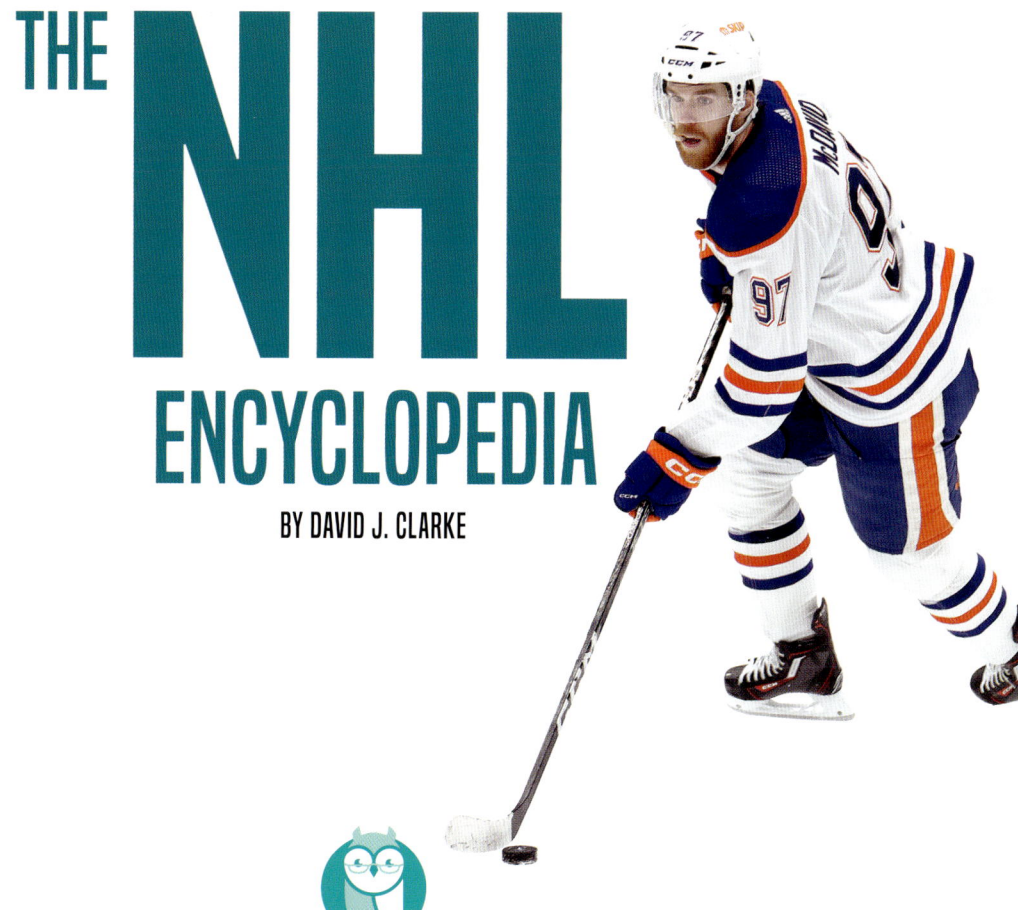

Encyclopedias
An Imprint of Abdo Reference
abdobooks.com

TABLE OF CONTENTS

THE HISTORY OF THE NATIONAL HOCKEY LEAGUE 4

NHL TEAMS 20
- Anaheim Ducks 20
- Boston Bruins 24
- Buffalo Sabres 28
- Calgary Flames 32
- Carolina Hurricanes 36
- Chicago Blackhawks 40
- Colorado Avalanche 44
- Columbus Blue Jackets 48
- Dallas Stars 52
- Detroit Red Wings 56
- Edmonton Oilers 60
- Florida Panthers 64
- Los Angeles Kings 68
- Minnesota Wild 72
- Montreal Canadiens 76
- Nashville Predators 80
- New Jersey Devils 84
- New York Islanders 88
- New York Rangers 92
- Ottawa Senators 96
- Philadelphia Flyers 100
- Pittsburgh Penguins 104
- San Jose Sharks 108
- Seattle Kraken 112
- St. Louis Blues 116
- Tampa Bay Lightning 120
- Toronto Maple Leafs 124
- Utah Hockey Club 128
- Vancouver Canucks 132
- Vegas Golden Knights 136
- Washington Capitals 140
- Winnipeg Jets 144

STAR PLAYERS 148
- Jean Béliveau 148
- Mike Bossy 148
- Ray Bourque 149
- Johnny Bower 150
- Martin Brodeur 150
- Chris Chelios 151
- Paul Coffey 152
- Sidney Crosby 152
- Pavel Datsyuk 153
- Marcel Dionne 154
- Ken Dryden 154
- Phil Esposito 155
- Tony Esposito 156
- Ron Francis 156
- Mike Gartner 157
- Bernie Geoffrion 158
- Wayne Gretzky 159
- Glenn Hall 160
- Doug Harvey 160
- Dominik Hašek 161
- Gordie Howe 162
- Bobby Hull 162
- Brett Hull 163
- Jaromír Jágr 164
- Patrick Kane 165
- Guy Lafleur 166
- Mario Lemieux 167
- Nicklas Lidström 168
- Ted Lindsay 168
- Connor McDavid 169
- Mark Messier 170
- Stan Mikita 170
- Mike Modano 171
- Howie Morenz 172
- Bobby Orr 173

Alex Ovechkin	174
Jacques Plante	174
Denis Potvin	175
Henri Richard	176
Maurice Richard	176
Larry Robinson	177
Patrick Roy	178
Joe Sakic	178
Serge Savard	179
Terry Sawchuk	180
Teemu Selänne	180
Eddie Shore	181
Peter Šťastný	182
Bryan Trottier	182
Steve Yzerman	183

HONORABLE MENTIONS	**184**
NHL ALL-TIME LEADERS	**186**
GLOSSARY	**188**
TO LEARN MORE	**189**
INDEX	**190**
PHOTO CREDITS	**191**

THE HISTORY OF THE
NATIONAL HOCKEY LEAGUE

The Montreal Wanderers played in three early hockey leagues before becoming a founding member of the NHL.

Millions of fans follow today's National Hockey League (NHL), which has 32 teams spread across North America. Each team plays in big, modern arenas, with the games being broadcast around the world. The league's origins more than a century ago were much more humble.

The National Hockey Association (NHA) was a Canadian hockey league that formed in 1910. By 1917, the NHA had five teams. The men who ran four of the teams strongly disliked their fifth partner, Eddie Livingstone. He ran the Toronto Shamrocks. The other owners thought Livingstone regularly broke league rules. So on November 26, 1917, they decided to leave him behind and create their own league. The new NHL was born. It had four teams: the Montreal Canadiens, Montreal Wanderers, Ottawa Senators, and Toronto Arenas.

The league got off to a troubling start. Just a few games into the 1917–18 season, the arena that the Canadiens and Wanderers shared burned down. The Canadiens found a new home, but the Wanderers stopped playing. The NHL's opening season finished with just three teams.

The league managed to survive and even grow. The Boston Bruins became the first team in the United States in 1924. Over the next few decades, the NHL added and lost teams regularly. At one point, the league had ten teams. However, only seven remained as the NHL entered the 1940s.

THE STANLEY CUP

The Stanley Cup is awarded each year to the NHL champion. But that wasn't always the case. The trophy is older than the league, having been created in 1892. In the NHL's earliest days, the league champion played the winner of the Pacific Coast Hockey Association (PCHA) for the trophy. After the PCHA folded, the NHL took over the Stanley Cup in 1926.

THE HISTORY OF THE NATIONAL HOCKEY LEAGUE

THE ORIGINAL SIX

At the end of the 1941–42 season, the New York Americans folded. That left the league with only six teams. These were the Boston Bruins, Chicago Black Hawks, Detroit Red Wings, Montreal Canadiens, New York Rangers, and Toronto Maple Leafs. Those six clubs would make up the NHL for the next 25 seasons. Later, after the league expanded, the group would come to be known as the Original Six.

In 1942, the Chicago Black Hawks featured brothers Reggie, Max, and Doug Bentley.

Many of the league's first big stars emerged during this era. Montreal winger Maurice Richard became the first NHL player to score 50 goals in a season in 1944–45. Gordie Howe joined the Red Wings in 1946. He went on to play a record 26 seasons in the NHL.

The Canadiens, Red Wings, and Maple Leafs dominated the Original Six era. The three teams built up talent by creating huge networks of minor league teams to feed them players. In the 25 years between the 1942–43 and 1966–67 seasons, the trio combined to win all but one Stanley Cup.

Black Hawks goaltender Charlie Gardiner, *left*, won the Vezina Trophy as the league's best goaltender in 1932.

By the late 1950s, many of the league's early builders were leaving the sport. Several are now honored with trophies named after them. Frank Calder was the NHL's first president. Now, the league's top rookie each season wins the Calder Trophy. The Jack Adams Award goes to the league's best coach. Adams led the Red Wings to three Stanley Cups before leaving the team in 1947. Awards such as the Art Ross Trophy (top scorer), Frank J. Selke Trophy (top defensive forward), and James Norris Trophy (top defenseman) are all named after men who helped create the early NHL.

Despite holding losing records, both the Los Angeles Kings and Minnesota North Stars reached the playoffs in their first NHL season.

THE NHL EXPANDS

In the mid-1960s, NHL owners decided to expand the league. Six new teams were added in the 1967–68 season. They included the Los Angeles Kings, Minnesota North Stars, Oakland Seals, Philadelphia Flyers, Pittsburgh Penguins, and St. Louis Blues.

The new teams were all placed in the league's new West Division. The Original Six teams made up the East Division. But the new teams had weaker rosters. This meant they had no chance when the division champions met for the Stanley Cup. The Blues won the West in each of their first three years. But the team lost all three Stanley Cup Final series without winning a single game.

The Buffalo Sabres and Vancouver Canucks both joined the NHL in the 1970–71 season. The NHL entered the 1970s larger than it had ever been before. But new challenges were right around the corner.

Gilbert Perreault was a star for the Buffalo Sabres in the club's early years.

Philadelphia's Bobby Clarke, *left*, and Bernie Parent, *right*, hold up the Stanley Cup after the Flyers' 1974 victory.

RIVALS AND DYNASTIES

The 1970s were a challenging decade for the NHL. The league kept growing, but the new teams often struggled to compete. Many of them lost money. Even worse, a new league had arrived to challenge the NHL for top players.

The World Hockey Association (WHA) formed in 1972. It promised big salaries to top NHL stars. Several players left the NHL for these bigger paychecks.

Meanwhile, three NHL teams dominated the decade. The Boston Bruins won two titles led by graceful, speedy defenseman Bobby Orr. The Philadelphia Flyers became the first non-Original Six team to win a championship in 1973–74.

However, the Montreal Canadiens soon outplayed the Flyers and dominated the rest of the decade. Montreal won six championships in the 1970s. By the end of the decade, the Canadiens had won a total of 21 Stanley Cups.

The end of the 1970s also saw the end of the WHA. The league struggled for money. Teams moved cities and folded every year. Finally, the two leagues decided to merge. The WHA stopped playing, and four of its teams joined the NHL. By the 1979–80 season, the NHL had grown to 21 teams.

CLARENCE CAMPBELL

Clarence Campbell became the NHL's president in 1946. He spent 31 years on the job and oversaw major expansion. From 1974 to 1993, what is now the Western Conference was known as the Campbell Conference. The winner of the Western Conference still receives the Clarence S. Campbell Bowl.

THE HISTORY OF THE NATIONAL HOCKEY LEAGUE

Right winger Mike Bossy was the top goal scorer on the Islanders' dynasty teams of the early 1980s.

NEW DYNASTIES

The 1980s were a new era for the NHL in many ways. The league was larger than ever before. And it looked very different. In the early days of the NHL, most players came from Canada. By the 1980s, many more Americans and Europeans were joining teams. With more talent in the league, games became higher scoring. New powers emerged.

The first was the New York Islanders. The team had only been founded in 1972. But by 1979–80 the Islanders started a run of four straight Stanley Cup titles. No team has won more than two straight since.

The Edmonton Oilers were one of the four WHA teams to join the NHL. In 1983–84, they beat the Islanders to claim their first title. In a high-scoring league, the Oilers were the flashiest team. They had several stars, but Wayne Gretzky led the way. Four times during the 1980s he scored 200 points in a season. No other player has ever reached that mark even once. And Gretzky led the Oilers to four Stanley Cups. Along the way, the Ontario native became a Canadian national hero.

However, after the 1987–88 season, Gretzky was traded to the Los Angeles Kings. The deal shocked the league. Members of the Canadian government even tried to stop the trade. Though many Canadians remained upset, Gretzky's move turned out to be great for the growth of the NHL.

Wayne Gretzky is the only player in NHL history to score more than 90 goals in a season. He tallied 92 in 1981–82.

THE HISTORY OF THE NATIONAL HOCKEY LEAGUE

HOCKEY GOES SOUTH

When fans flocked to Kings games to watch Gretzky, the NHL realized it could reach new markets. The Kings had been around since 1967. But the league's other 20 teams were in northern US cities or in Canada. In the early 1990s, a new round of expansion teams brought the league farther south. The Tampa Bay Lightning and Florida Panthers were the first two NHL teams in Florida. The San Jose Sharks and the Anaheim Mighty Ducks began playing in California.

The Florida Panthers select players at the NHL Expansion Draft in 1993.

Many struggling NHL teams also moved cities during the decade. The Minnesota North Stars moved to Dallas and became the Stars. The Winnipeg Jets relocated to Phoenix and became the Coyotes. The Quebec Nordiques moved to Denver and were renamed the Colorado Avalanche. Finally, the Hartford Whalers moved to Raleigh and became the Carolina Hurricanes.

The game was changing on the ice as well. Gone were the high-flying, high-scoring 1980s. By the late 1990s, goalie equipment was becoming bigger, helping them stop shots. Teams were also clamping down by playing physical defense, often by holding and hooking forwards. The era became known as the NHL's "clutch and grab" period.

Despite the lower-scoring games, the NHL continued to grow. The Nashville Predators began play in time for the 1998–99 season. The next year, the Atlanta Thrashers joined the league. In 2000–01, the Columbus Blue Jackets arrived, as did a new franchise in Minnesota called the Wild. By the early 2000s, the 30-team NHL was bigger than ever. But it was also headed for disaster.

A CANCELED SEASON

As the NHL grew, it had a big problem. In the early 2000s, the rich teams were able to spend money on players that the less wealthy teams could not. The owners' solution was to put a salary limit on player contracts. That way each team could spend the same amount. However, players thought the owners were just trying to keep them from making more money. They refused to allow the cap.

A GLOBAL GAME

In 1980, 82.2 percent of NHL players were from Canada, while another 11.2 percent were from the United States. Since then, the league has become far more global. In 2023, just 41.7 percent of players were Canadian. US-born players made up 29.1 percent, while 9.1 percent came from Sweden. Russia, Finland, and the Czech Republic all contributed at least 3 percent of NHL players as well.

THE HISTORY OF THE NATIONAL HOCKEY LEAGUE

NHL fans, including those attending other sporting events, showed their frustration with the canceled 2004–05 season.

The argument became so heated that before the 2004–05 season, the owners decided on a lockout. They would prevent the players from coming to work until a new deal was made. Many NHL stars quickly signed with European teams while they waited for the NHL to return. However, after negotiations failed, the NHL season was canceled. No North American sports league had ever wiped out an entire season before. Some frustrated fans vowed never to watch the NHL again.

The players eventually agreed to a salary cap, and the NHL returned in 2005–06. There were also many new rules designed to bring scoring back. Offensive zones were made bigger so players would have more room. Goalies were restricted in where they could handle the puck. And referees were told to call more penalties when players hooked and held opponents.

The biggest rule change was that the league eliminated tie games. Previously, games that remained even through an overtime period were recorded as ties. Under the new rules, teams settled tie games with overtime followed by penalty shot shoot-outs featuring one player on the ice in a breakaway against the goaltender. Critics didn't like the change. But shoot-outs are still used in the NHL today.

A new wave of stars, led by Pittsburgh Penguins center Sidney Crosby and Washington Capitals winger Alex Ovechkin, took over the league. Games slowly became higher scoring. And fans eventually returned to the arenas.

The addition of shoot-outs in the 2005–06 season was a significant change to NHL rules.

HOCKEY BOOM

Some individual teams struggled after the lockout. But big television contracts helped the league become more profitable than ever. Even another lockout that wiped out half the 2012–13 season didn't stop the NHL's progress.

The new salary cap created a more competitive league. No teams dominated like they had in the past, but there were still dynasties. In 2009–10, the Chicago Blackhawks won their first Stanley Cup in nearly 50 years. Chicago won twice more in the next five years. The Los Angeles Kings, Pittsburgh Penguins, and Tampa Bay Lightning all won multiple championships in the 2010s and 2020s.

Jonathan Toews was the captain of the Blackhawks' championship teams in the 2010s.

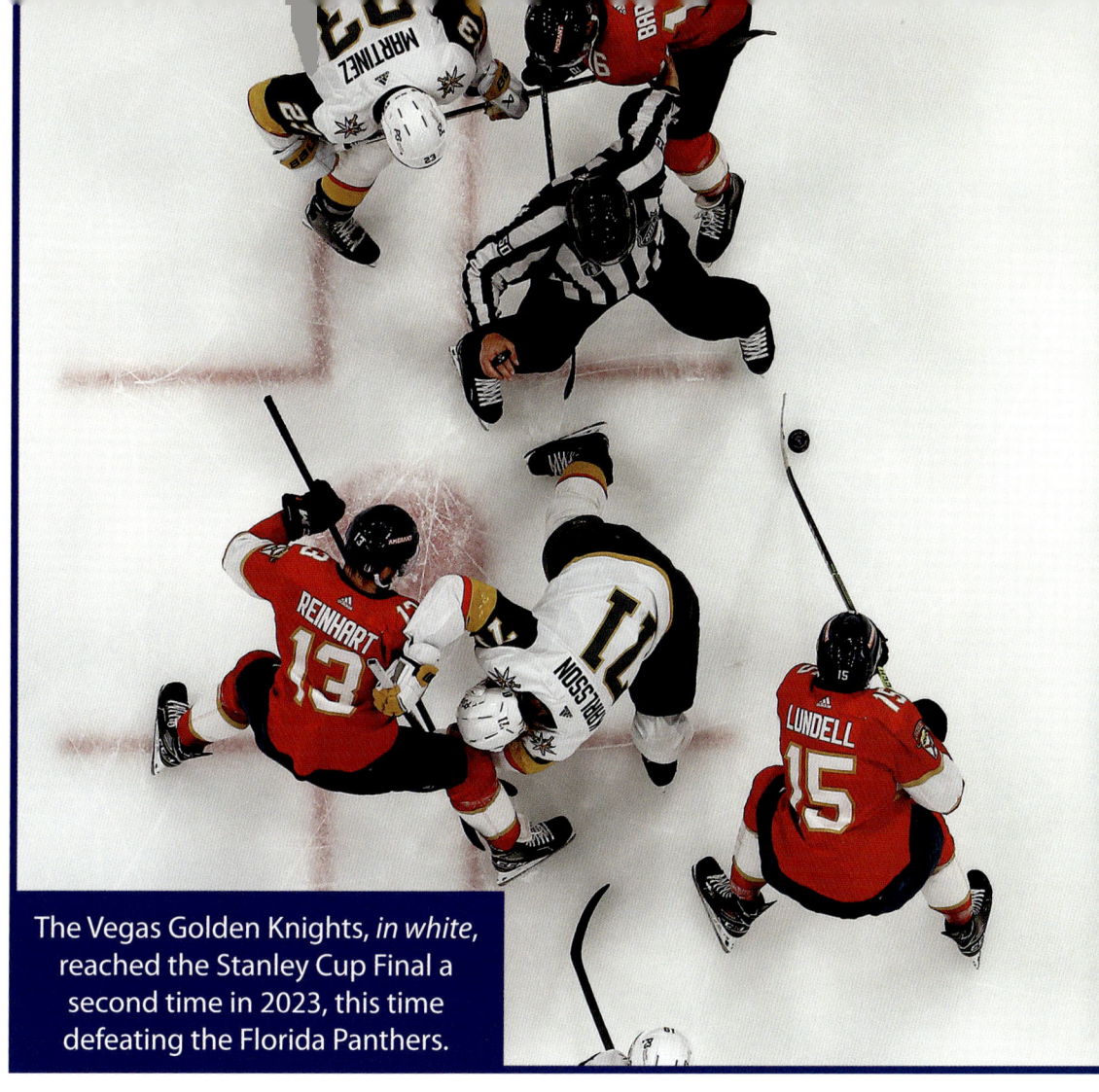

The Vegas Golden Knights, *in white*, reached the Stanley Cup Final a second time in 2023, this time defeating the Florida Panthers.

    Another trend that continued into the 2000s was a lack of Stanley Cup championships for Canadian teams. Montreal won in 1992–93. Over the next 30 seasons, no Canadian team claimed the Cup. Meanwhile, two new teams arrived in the United States in another round of expansion. The Vegas Golden Knights joined the NHL in 2017–18. The team was instantly successful, reaching the Stanley Cup Final in its first season. The Seattle Kraken became the NHL's thirty-second team in 2021–22. They reached the playoffs in just their second season.

ANAHEIM DUCKS

The Anaheim Ducks retired Finnish star Teemu Selänne's No. 8 jersey in 2015.

TEAM HISTORY

The Anaheim Ducks formed in 1993. The team's first owner was the Walt Disney Company. The year before, Disney had released the film *The Mighty Ducks*. The team took its name from the movie and played its first 12 seasons as the Mighty

Ducks of Anaheim. Disney sold the team in 2005. The new owners changed the team's colors from teal and purple to orange and black. They also shortened the name to the Anaheim Ducks. In the first season of their new ownership, the Ducks won their first Stanley Cup.

GREATEST PLAYERS

- **Cam Fowler**, D (2010–)
- **Ryan Getzlaf**, C (2005–22)
- **John Gibson**, G (2014–)
- **Jean-Sébastien Giguère**, G (2000–10)
- **Guy Hebert**, G (1993–2001)
- **Jonas Hiller**, G (2007–14)
- **Paul Kariya**, LW (1994–2003)
- **Scott Niedermayer**, D (2006–10)
- **Corey Perry**, RW (2005–19)
- **Chris Pronger**, D (2006–09)
- **Steve Rucchin**, C (1995–2004)
- **Teemu Selänne**, RW (1996–2001, 2005–14)

GIGUÈRE'S HEROICS

In 2003, Jean-Sébastien Giguère put together one of the most memorable postseasons in NHL history. He allowed an average of 1.62 goals per game and stopped a then-record 94.5 percent of the shots he faced. In the Western Conference finals against the Minnesota Wild, Giguère recorded shutouts in each of the first three games. Anaheim lost that year's Stanley Cup to the New Jersey Devils. But Giguère was awarded the Conn Smythe Trophy as the playoffs' Most Valuable Player (MVP). He was just the fifth player from a losing team to earn the award.

TEAM STATS AND RECORDS*

ALL-TIME RECORD
- **Regular season (Wins–Losses–Ties–Overtime losses):** 1071–968–107–211
- **Postseason:** 89–73
- **Stanley Cup Final record:** 1–1

TOP COACHES
- **Randy Carlyle** (2006–12, 2016–19); 384–256–N/A–96 (regular season); 46–37 (postseason)
- **Bruce Boudreau** (2012–2016); 208–104–N/A–40 (regular season); 24–19 (postseason)

CAREER OFFENSIVE LEADERS
- **Games played:** Ryan Getzlaf, 1,157
- **Goals:** Teemu Selänne, 457
- **Assists:** Ryan Getzlaf, 737
- **Points:** Ryan Getzlaf, 1,019
- **Penalty minutes:** Corey Perry, 1,110
- **Hat tricks:** Teemu Selänne, 13
- **Shorthanded goals:** Paul Kariya/Andrew Cogliano, 16
- **Power play goals:** Teemu Selänne, 182
- **Game-winning goals:** Teemu Selänne, 77

Jean-Sébastien Giguère was drafted by the Hartford Whalers in 1995 and joined the Ducks five years later.

Travis Moen, *right*, celebrates his Stanley Cup–clinching goal in game 5 of the 2007 Final. The bizarre goal was credited to Moen after Chris Phillips of the Ottawa Senators accidentally put the puck in his own net.

CAREER GOALTENDING LEADERS
- **Games played**: John Gibson, 477
- **Wins**: Jean-Sébastien Giguère, 206
- **Goals against average**: Frederik Andersen, 2.33
- **Save percentage**: Frederik Andersen, .918
- **Shutouts**: Jean-Sébastien Giguère, 32

*All statistics and records in this book are through 2023–24.

GREATEST SEASONS

In 2002–03, Anaheim was just the No. 7 seed in the Western Conference. Behind the stellar goaltending of Jean-Sébastien Giguère, the Ducks reached the Stanley Cup Final. However, they lost in a tight seven-game series against the New Jersey Devils.

Three years later, the Ducks finished with team records of 48 wins and 110 points. Coach Randy Carlyle's group then steamrolled the competition in the playoffs. The Ducks beat the Minnesota Wild, Vancouver Canucks, and Detroit Red Wings on their way to the Stanley Cup Final against the Ottawa Senators. Anaheim then beat the Senators 4–1 to capture their first championship.

BOSTON BRUINS

The Bruins won three Stanley Cups in their first few decades of existence.

TEAM HISTORY

Founded in 1924, the Boston Bruins became the first NHL team based in the United States. For most of their history, the Bruins have been contenders, but championships haven't always been easy to come by. Boston's six Stanley Cups are tied for fourth-most of any NHL team, but the Bruins have also lost a league-high 14 Stanley Cup Final series.

The team won three times in their first 17 seasons. Then the Bruins waited another 29 years before stars Bobby Orr and Phil Esposito led the team to glory in 1969–70 and 1971–72. From there, it was a long wait before Boston won again in 2010–11.

GREATEST PLAYERS

- **Patrice Bergeron**, C (2003–23)
- **Ray Bourque**, D (1979–2000)
- **Johnny Bucyk**, LW (1957–78)
- **Dit Clapper**, RW/D (1927–47)
- **Phil Esposito**, C (1967–75)
- **Rick Middleton**, RW (1976–88)
- **Cam Neely**, RW (1986–96)
- **Terry O'Reilly**, RW (1971–85)
- **Bobby Orr**, D (1966–76)
- **Tuukka Rask**, G (2007, 2009–22)
- **Milt Schmidt**, C/D (1936–55)
- **Eddie Shore**, D (1926–40)

Ray Bourque was drafted by Boston in 1979 and went on to play more than 1,500 games for the team.

TEAM STATS AND RECORDS

ALL-TIME RECORD
- **Regular season:** 3404–2461–791–216
- **Postseason:** 344–352
- **Stanley Cup Final record:** 6–14

TOP COACHES
- **Art Ross** (1924–45); 387–290–95–N/A (regular season); 32–33–5 (postseason)
- **Claude Julien** (2007–17); 419–246–N/A–94 (regular season); 57–40 (postseason)

CAREER OFFENSIVE LEADERS
- **Games played:** Ray Bourque, 1,518
- **Goals:** Johnny Bucyk, 545
- **Assists:** Ray Bourque, 1,111
- **Points:** Ray Bourque, 1,506
- **Penalty minutes:** Terry O'Reilly, 2,095
- **Hat tricks:** Phil Esposito, 26
- **Shorthanded goals:** Brad Marchand, 36
- **Power play goals:** Ray Bourque, 164
- **Game-winning goals:** Johnny Bucyk, 88

CAREER GOALTENDING LEADERS
- **Games played:** Tuukka Rask, 564
- **Wins:** Tuukka Rask, 308
- **Goals against average:** Tiny Thompson, 1.99
- **Save percentage:** Linus Ullmark, .924
- **Shutouts:** Tiny Thompson, 74

THE HARD WAY

The 2010–11 Bruins had to survive a very long playoff run. They beat the Montreal Canadiens and the Tampa Bay Lightning in seven games each. Boston then captured the Stanley Cup in seven against the Vancouver Canucks. No team had ever won three seven-game series in the same playoffs before.

Photographer Ray Lussier captured the famous photo of Bobby Orr flying through the air after winning the 1970 Stanley Cup Final.

GREATEST SEASONS

Bobby Orr scored in overtime of game 4 to seal the 1970 Stanley Cup for Boston. He was tripped as he shot the puck and went flying through the air with his arms extended in celebration. A photograph of the moment became one of the most famous pictures in American sports history. The win also started a mini dynasty for the Bruins. Two years later, the team won 54 regular-season games and captured another Stanley Cup.

BUFFALO SABRES

TEAM HISTORY

The Buffalo Sabres entered the NHL as an expansion team in 1970. Within five seasons, the team's line of Gilbert Perreault, Rick Martin, and René Robert brought Buffalo to its first Stanley Cup Final appearance. The Sabres lost that series to the Philadelphia Flyers.

Buffalo also lost its only other Final appearance in 1999 to the Dallas Stars. In the 2000s, the Sabres have mostly been known for losing in the regular season. In 2023–24, Buffalo missed the playoffs for the thirteenth straight year.

The line of René Robert, *left*, Gilbert Perreault, *center*, and Rick Martin, *right*, was nicknamed the "French Connection."

A LUCKY SPIN

Before the Sabres and Vancouver Canucks entered the NHL together in 1970, they faced off in a lottery spin for that year's top draft pick. Everyone knew the first pick would be young star Gilbert Perreault. A league official spun a wheel with 20 numbers on it. Numbers one through ten belonged to Vancouver, and Buffalo had 11 through 20. The wheel stopped on 11, and the Sabres got Perreault, who went on to become a team icon.

GREATEST PLAYERS

- **Dave Andreychuk**, LW (1982–93, 2000–01)
- **Danny Gare**, RW (1974–81)
- **Dominik Hašek**, G (1992–2001)
- **Phil Housley**, D (1982–90)
- **Pat LaFontaine**, C (1991–97)
- **Rick Martin**, LW (1971–81)
- **Ryan Miller**, G (2002–14)
- **Gilbert Perreault**, C (1970–87)
- **Craig Ramsay**, LW (1971–85)
- **Mike Ramsey**, D (1980–92)
- **Rob Ray**, RW (1989–2003)
- **René Robert**, RW (1971–79)

Lindy Ruff played for the Sabres in the 1980s. In 2024, he began his second stint as Buffalo's head coach.

TEAM STATS AND RECORDS

ALL-TIME RECORD
- **Regular season:** 1918–1673–409–191
- **Postseason:** 124–132
- **Stanley Cup Final record:** 0–2

TOP COACHES
- **Scotty Bowman** (1979–80, 1981–87); 210–134–60–N/A (regular season); 18–18 (postseason)
- **Lindy Ruff** (1997–2013, 2024–); 571–432–78–84 (regular season); 57–44 (postseason)

CAREER OFFENSIVE LEADERS
- **Games played:** Gilbert Perreault, 1,191
- **Goals:** Gilbert Perreault, 512
- **Assists:** Gilbert Perreault, 814
- **Points:** Gilbert Perreault, 1,326
- **Penalty minutes:** Rob Ray, 3,189
- **Hat tricks:** Rick Martin, 21
- **Shorthanded goals:** Craig Ramsay, 27
- **Power play goals:** Dave Andreychuk, 161
- **Game-winning goals:** Gilbert Perreault, 81

CAREER GOALTENDING LEADERS
- **Games played:** Ryan Miller, 540
- **Wins:** Ryan Miller, 284
- **Goals against average:** Dominik Hašek, 2.22
- **Save percentage:** Dominik Hašek, .926
- **Shutouts:** Dominik Hašek, 55

The Sabres' Jim Schoenfeld, *right*, moves toward the Flyers' goal during the 1975 "Fog Game."

GREATEST SEASONS

Along the way to the 1975 Stanley Cup Final, the Sabres won one of the strangest games in NHL history. Buffalo's arena did not have air conditioning. The hot, humid weather created a layer of fog on the rink as the players took the ice for game 3 of the series. The players could barely see their own feet.

Play was stopped several times so arena staff could attempt to clear the fog, but nothing worked. A bat was also flying around the arena during the game. Before a face-off in the first period, Sabres center Jim Lorentz knocked the bat out of the air with his stick. In the end, Buffalo won the "Fog Game" 5–4 in overtime on a goal by René Robert.

CALGARY FLAMES

Curt Bennett played for the Atlanta Flames during the team's first several years in the league.

TEAM HISTORY

The Calgary Flames began as an expansion team in 1972–73. But the team originally played far from Calgary, Alberta. The team was founded as the Atlanta Flames. After struggling financially in Georgia for eight seasons, the Flames moved north.

In the 1980s, they developed a fierce rivalry with the Edmonton Oilers, Calgary's provincial neighbors. To this day, the heated games are known as Battles of Alberta. But while the Oilers were a dominant team in that decade, the

Flames kept coming up just short. Calgary lost the Stanley Cup Final to Montreal in 1986. It finally broke through three years later for the Flames' only championship. Despite a surprise run to the Final in 2004, the years since have been mostly lean as the team has struggled to develop consistent stars.

GREATEST PLAYERS

- **Theo Fleury**, RW (1988–99)
- **Johnny Gaudreau**, LW (2014–22)
- **Mark Giordano**, D (2006–21)
- **Jarome Iginla**, RW (1996–2013)
- **Miikka Kiprusoff**, G (2003–13)
- **Al MacInnis**, D (1981–94)
- **Lanny McDonald**, RW (1981–89)
- **Joe Nieuwendyk**, C (1986–95)
- **Robyn Regehr**, D (1999–2011)
- **Gary Roberts**, LW (1986–96)
- **Gary Suter**, D (1985–94)
- **Mike Vernon**, G (1982, 1984–94, 2000–02)

LANNY McDONALD

Lanny McDonald was a hugely popular star for the Flames throughout the 1980s. But in the 1989 playoffs, he was 36 years old and nearing retirement. In game 6 of the Stanley Cup Final against the Montreal Canadiens, McDonald stepped out of the penalty box and raced up ice to score his only goal of the playoffs. Calgary went on to win the game 4–2 and clinch its only Stanley Cup. McDonald's goal is remembered as one of the most emotional moments in NHL history.

CALGARY FLAMES

TEAM STATS AND RECORDS

ALL-TIME RECORD
- **Regular season:** 1891–1583–379–183
- **Postseason:** 110–140
- **Stanley Cup Final record:** 1–2

TOP COACHES
- **Terry Crisp** (1988–90); 144–63–33–N/A (regular season); 22–15 (postseason)
- **Darryl Sutter** (2002–06, 2021–23); 210–136–15–43 (regular season); 23–22 (postseason)

CAREER OFFENSIVE LEADERS
- **Games played:** Jarome Iginla, 1,219
- **Goals:** Jarome Iginla, 525
- **Assists:** Al MacInnis, 609
- **Points:** Jarome Iginla, 1,095
- **Penalty minutes:** Tim Hunter, 2,405
- **Hat tricks:** Kent Nilsson, 14
- **Shorthanded goals:** Theo Fleury, 28
- **Power play goals:** Jarome Iginla, 161
- **Game-winning goals:** Jarome Iginla, 83

CAREER GOALTENDING LEADERS
- **Games played:** Miikka Kiprusoff, 576
- **Wins:** Miikka Kiprusoff, 305
- **Goals against average:** Miikka Kiprusoff, 2.46
- **Save percentage:** Miikka Kiprusoff, .913
- **Shutouts:** Miikka Kiprusoff, 41

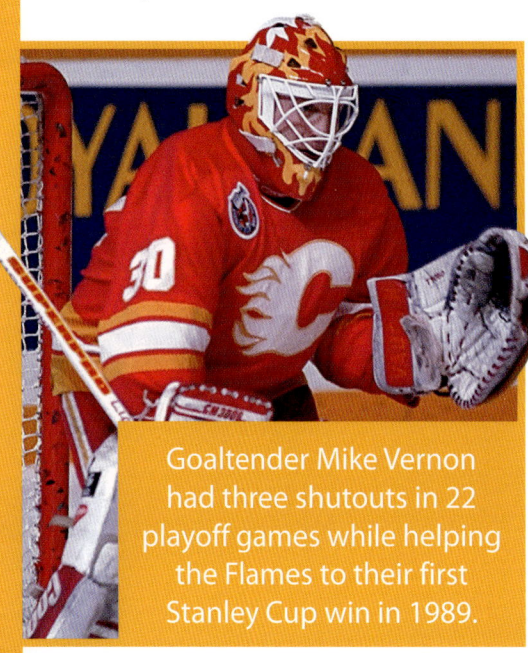

Goaltender Mike Vernon had three shutouts in 22 playoff games while helping the Flames to their first Stanley Cup win in 1989.

Lanny McDonald, *holding trophy*, and the 1989 Calgary Flames celebrate their Stanley Cup win.

GREATEST SEASONS

The Flames reached the playoffs every season in the 1980s, but they consistently failed to win. Calgary finally found success in 1988–89. The team won a record 54 games, then survived an upset attempt by the Vancouver Canucks in the first round of the playoffs. Calgary winger Joel Otto's overtime goal in game 7 pushed the Flames to the next round.

Calgary eventually outlasted the Montreal Canadiens in six games to win the team's first Stanley Cup championship. Defenseman Al MacInnis led the way. His seven goals and 24 assists in the playoffs earned him the Conn Smythe Trophy.

CAROLINA HURRICANES

Ron Francis spent 16 of his 23 NHL seasons with the Hartford Whalers/Carolina Hurricanes after the franchise drafted him in 1981. He was also the team's general manager from 2014 to 2018.

TEAM HISTORY

The Hurricanes began their hockey life in the WHA. They played their games in Boston and were known as the New England Whalers. After a few seasons, the team moved to Hartford, Connecticut, but they kept the Whalers nickname. Later, Hartford became one of four teams that moved to the NHL after the WHA folded.

The team had been successful in the WHA, but life in the NHL was tough for the Whalers. Hartford was the smallest city in the league, and many fans in the area already rooted for the nearby Boston Bruins or the two New York–area teams. After nearly two decades of struggle, the Whalers moved to Raleigh, North Carolina, in 1997 and were renamed the Hurricanes. Carolina reached the Stanley Cup Final twice in its first decade in Raleigh. The Hurricanes won their only title in 2005–06.

The team experienced a downturn after that. But a group of exciting young players turned Carolina into a contender again in the early 2020s. And the team's postgame celebrations after home wins created a unique identity for the Hurricanes.

GREATEST PLAYERS

- **Sebastian Aho**, C (2016–)
- **Rod Brind'Amour**, C (2000–10)
- **Sean Burke**, G (1992–98)
- **Kevin Dineen**, RW (1984–91, 1995–99)
- **Ron Francis**, C (1981–91, 1998–2004)
- **Artūrs Irbe**, G (1998–2004)
- **Jeff O'Neill**, RW (1995–2004)
- **Jaccob Slavin**, D (2015–)
- **Eric Staal**, C (2003–16)
- **Jordan Staal**, C (2012–)
- **Cam Ward**, G (2005–18)
- **Glen Wesley**, D (1994–2008)

Rod Brind'Amour steals the puck and scores to secure a win with 32 seconds remaining in game 1 of the 2006 Stanley Cup Final.

TEAM STATS AND RECORDS

ALL-TIME RECORD
- **Regular season:** 1519–1498–263–198
- **Postseason:** 97–104
- **Stanley Cup Final record:** 1–1

TOP COACHES
- **Peter Laviolette** (2004–09); 167–122–6–28 (regular season); 16–9 (postseason)
- **Rod Brind'Amour** (2019–); 278–130–N/A–44 (regular season); 38–36 (postseason)

CAREER OFFENSIVE LEADERS
- **Games played:** Ron Francis, 1,186
- **Goals:** Ron Francis, 382
- **Assists:** Ron Francis, 793
- **Points:** Ron Francis, 1,175
- **Penalty minutes:** Kevin Dineen, 1,439
- **Hat tricks:** Eric Staal, 13
- **Shorthanded goals:** Sebastian Aho, 17
- **Power play goals:** Ron Francis, 132
- **Game-winning goals:** Ron Francis, 57

CAREER GOALTENDING LEADERS
- **Games played:** Cam Ward, 668
- **Wins:** Cam Ward, 318
- **Goals against average:** Frederik Andersen, 2.22
- **Save percentage:** Frederik Andersen, .918
- **Shutouts:** Cam Ward, 27

GREATEST SEASONS

Not much was expected of the Hurricanes when they reached the playoffs in 2001–02. The team had won only 35 of its 82 regular-season games. But behind stellar play from Latvian goaltender Artūrs Irbe, Carolina upset the defending champion New Jersey Devils in the first round. The Hurricanes reached the Stanley Cup Final before losing to the Detroit Red Wings.

The Hurricanes circle up to perform a Storm Surge celebration after defeating the Los Angeles Kings in a 2023 game.

Four years later, another goaltender led a deep playoff run. Rookie Cam Ward had struggled during the regular season. But Ward caught fire in the postseason, posting a 2.14 goals against average and two shutouts. Carolina nearly blew a 3–1 lead in the Stanley Cup Final. But forward Justin Williams sealed the Stanley Cup win over the Edmonton Oilers in the seventh game by scoring an empty-net goal with 1:01 left.

STORM SURGE

NHL teams often skate to center ice after wins to salute their fans. Often, players will hold their sticks up. But the Carolina Hurricanes decided to take the tradition a step further in 2019–20. The team started performing choreographed celebrations called Storm Surges. They could be anything from one of the players bowling his helmet at teammates, who acted as pins, to performing a limbo under a hockey stick. Fans loved the creativity, and the team has kept the tradition going.

CHICAGO BLACKHAWKS

Johnny Gottselig, *14*, of the Chicago Black Hawks tries to score against the Montreal Maroons in a 1929 game.

TEAM HISTORY

Chicago's NHL history has been a roller-coaster ride. Founded in 1926, the team won two Stanley Cups in the 1930s. Then it sank out of contention for most of the next two decades. And despite reaching the playoffs in all but one season between 1958–59 and 1996–97, Chicago won only one title.

Then, following years of struggles, the Blackhawks emerged as a dominant force in 2009–10. The team was led by star forwards Patrick Kane and Jonathan Toews as well as defenseman Duncan Keith. A Stanley Cup title that year kicked off a stretch of three championships in six seasons.

After another losing period, a new hope arrived in the 2023 draft. With the top pick, the Blackhawks selected gifted forward Connor Bedard. The much-hyped prospect won the Calder Trophy, and fans hoped for another golden age to come.

GREATEST PLAYERS

- **Chris Chelios**, D (1990–99)
- **Tony Esposito**, G (1969–84)
- **Glenn Hall**, G (1957–67)
- **Bobby Hull**, LW (1957–72)
- **Patrick Kane**, RW (2007–23)
- **Duncan Keith**, D (2005–21)
- **Steve Larmer**, RW (1981–93)
- **Stan Mikita**, C/RW (1958–80)
- **Pierre Pilote**, D (1956–68)
- **Denis Savard**, C (1980–90, 1995–97)
- **Jonathan Toews**, C (2007–23)
- **Doug Wilson**, D (1977–91)

NAMING MISTAKE

Chicago's NHL team was named after original owner Frederic McLaughlin's army unit in World War I (1914–18), which was known as the "Blackhawk" Division. But for nearly 60 years, the hockey team's nickname was mistakenly spelled as two words—Black Hawks. The error wasn't corrected until 1986, when the original team paperwork showed it should be simply one word.

TEAM STATS AND RECORDS

ALL-TIME RECORD
- **Regular season:** 2889–2905–814–198
- **Postseason:** 268–275
- **Stanley Cup Final record:** 6–7

TOP COACHES
- **Billy Reay** (1963–77); 516–335–161–N/A (regular season); 57–60 (postseason)
- **Joel Quenneville** (2008–19); 452–249–N/A–96 (regular season); 76–52 (postseason)

CAREER OFFENSIVE LEADERS
- **Games played:** Stan Mikita, 1,396
- **Goals:** Bobby Hull, 604
- **Assists:** Stan Mikita, 926
- **Points:** Stan Mikita, 1,467
- **Penalty minutes:** Chris Chelios, 1,495
- **Hat tricks:** Bobby Hull, 28
- **Shorthanded goals:** Dirk Graham, 26
- **Power play goals:** Steve Larmer, 153
- **Game-winning goals:** Bobby Hull, 98

CAREER GOALTENDING LEADERS
- **Games played:** Tony Esposito, 873
- **Wins:** Tony Esposito, 418
- **Goals against average:** Charlie Gardiner, 2.02
- **Save percentage:** Scott Darling, .923
- **Shutouts:** Tony Esposito, 74

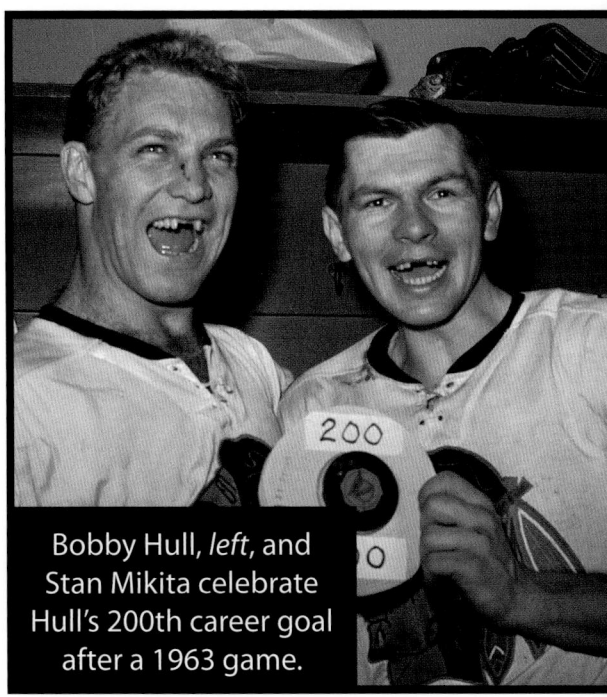

Bobby Hull, *left*, and Stan Mikita celebrate Hull's 200th career goal after a 1963 game.

GREATEST SEASONS

By 1960–61, the Detroit Red Wings, Montreal Canadiens, and Toronto Maple Leafs had won a combined 19 straight Stanley Cup titles. But the Black Hawks broke the streak by beating the Canadiens in the semifinals and then Detroit in the Final. They were led by stars Stan Mikita, Bobby Hull, Pierre Pilote, and goalie Glenn Hall.

Chicago didn't win another title until 2009–10. That year, the Blackhawks defeated the Philadelphia Flyers in overtime of game 6 to clinch the Stanley Cup. The winning goal was a curious one. Patrick Kane's shot went past Flyers' goaltender Michael Leighton, and the puck became stuck under the padding at the base of the net. It seemed like only Kane knew it had gone in. He was halfway down the ice in celebration before the other players and the officials figured out Chicago had won the game.

Patrick Kane jumps into the arms of goaltender Antti Niemi after scoring the overtime game-winning goal in game 6 of the 2010 Stanley Cup Final.

COLORADO AVALANCHE

TEAM HISTORY

The Colorado Avalanche began life as the Quebec Nordiques of the WHA. They joined the NHL in 1979. After many seasons in Quebec City, the team was sold to a group of owners in Denver. The newly named Avalanche began play in 1995–96 as one of the NHL's most talented teams. And they brought the Stanley Cup to Denver in their first season. The star-studded lineup continued to contend for titles. In 2000–01, a talented team that included multiple future Hall of Fame players added another Cup victory. During that era, the Avalanche enjoyed a heated rivalry with the West's other great team, the Detroit Red Wings. In the 2010s, the Avalanche assembled another roster of exciting young players including Nathan MacKinnon, Cale Makar, and Mikko Rantanen. This group led Colorado to the top again after the 2021–22 season, adding a third Stanley Cup to the team's trophy case.

The Avalanche drafted Nathan MacKinnon No. 1 overall in the 2013 NHL Draft.

GREATEST PLAYERS

- **Adam Foote**, D (1991–04, 2008–11)
- **Peter Forsberg**, C (1994–2004, 2008, 2011)
- **Michel Goulet**, LW (1979–90)
- **Milan Hejduk**, RW (1998–2013)
- **Gabriel Landeskog**, LW (2011–)
- **Nathan MacKinnon**, C (2013–)
- **Cale Makar**, D (2019–)
- **Mikko Rantanen**, RW (2015–)
- **Patrick Roy**, G (1995–2003)
- **Joe Sakic**, C (1988–2009)
- **Peter Šťastný**, C (1980–90)

Joe Sakic played his entire career for the Nordiques/Avalanche.

COLORADO AVALANCHE

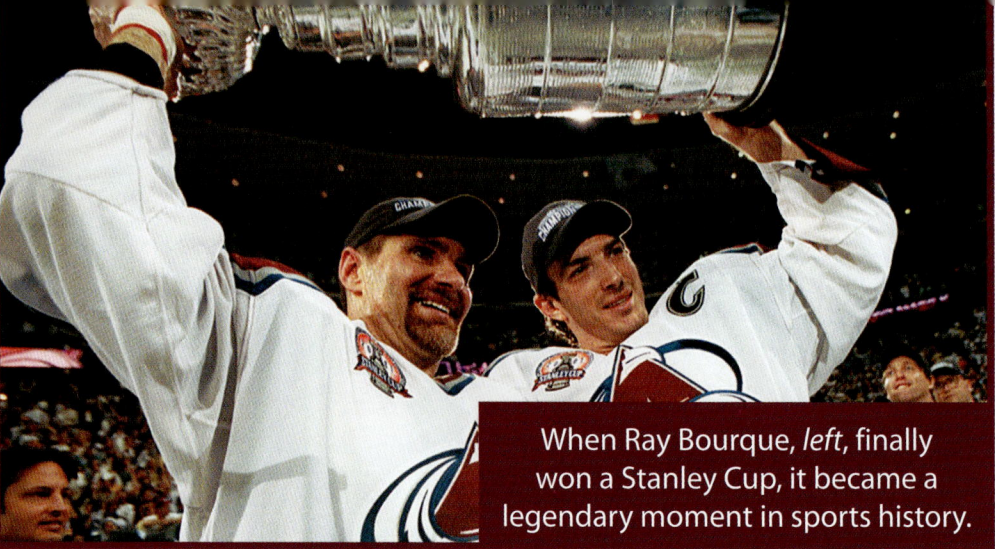

When Ray Bourque, *left*, finally won a Stanley Cup, it became a legendary moment in sports history.

TEAM STATS AND RECORDS

ALL-TIME RECORD
- **Regular season:** 1661–1395–261–163
- **Postseason:** 184–153
- **Stanley Cup Final record:** 3–3

TOP COACHES
- **Bob Hartley** (1998–2003); 193–108–48–10 (regular season); 49–31 (postseason)
- **Jared Bednar** (2016–); 341–217–N/A–60 (regular season); 49–32 (postseason)

CAREER OFFENSIVE LEADERS
- **Games played:** Joe Sakic, 1,378
- **Goals:** Joe Sakic, 625
- **Assists:** Joe Sakic, 1,016
- **Points:** Joe Sakic, 1,641
- **Penalty minutes:** Dale Hunter, 1,562
- **Hat tricks:** Peter Šťastný, 16
- **Shorthanded goals:** Joe Sakic, 32
- **Power play goals:** Joe Sakic, 205
- **Game-winning goals:** Joe Sakic, 86

CAREER GOALTENDING LEADERS
- **Games played:** Patrick Roy, 478
- **Wins:** Patrick Roy, 262
- **Goals against average:** Patrick Roy, 2.27
- **Save percentage:** Philipp Grubauer, .918
- **Shutouts:** Patrick Roy, 37

GREATEST SEASONS

The 1996 Stanley Cup Final was a four-game sweep by the Avalanche over the Florida Panthers. But game 4 was a marathon. The game was still scoreless 4:31 into the third overtime when Colorado defenseman Uwe Krupp blasted in a slap shot from the blue line to win the title.

Five years later, another defenseman led a memorable Cup run in Colorado. Legendary defenseman Ray Bourque had spent his first 20 NHL seasons in Boston without a championship before joining the Avalanche midway through his twenty-first season in 1999–2000. He was one of the league's most respected and well-liked players. Bourque's quest for the Cup finally ended the following season when the Avalanche outlasted the New Jersey Devils in seven games. Colorado captain Joe Sakic had barely touched the Cup when he handed it over to Bourque for an emotional ceremonial lap around the rink.

REJECTION PAYS OFF

In 1991, the Nordiques selected Eric Lindros with the first pick in the NHL Draft. Lindros was considered a future superstar, and he did not want to play in Quebec City. The Nordiques eventually traded him to the Philadelphia Flyers for $15 million, five players, and a future draft pick. Lindros did end up being a star, but the trade helped build the Avalanche dynasty. One of the players from the deal, center Peter Forsberg, became a Hall of Fame player in Colorado.

COLUMBUS BLUE JACKETS

The Blue Jackets struggled in their early seasons, but they still had talented players, including left winger Rick Nash.

TEAM HISTORY

The Columbus Blue Jackets joined the NHL as an expansion team in 2000. Over the next two decades, the team struggled to win. In 2006–07, the Blue Jackets were shut out 16 times in one season. That was the most of any NHL team since 1928–29. Columbus didn't record a winning season or reach the playoffs until 2008–09. The team didn't win a postseason game until 2013–14.

The team eventually found some playoff success, including a stunning series win over the Tampa Bay Lightning in 2018–19. But the Blue Jackets struggled to hold on to their star players, breaking apart a team that reached the playoffs four straight seasons. The 2023–24 season marked the fourth straight year outside the postseason in Columbus. It also marked the ninth time the team had finished last in its division in 23 seasons. In that time the Blue Jackets made the playoffs only six times.

GREATEST PLAYERS

- **Cam Atkinson**, RW (2011–21)
- **Sergei Bobrovsky**, G (2012–19)
- **Nick Foligno**, LW (2013–21)
- **Boone Jenner**, C (2013–)
- **Seth Jones**, D (2016–21)
- **Rostislav Klesla**, D (2000–11)
- **Steve Mason**, G (2008–13)
- **Rick Nash**, LW (2002–12)
- **David Savard**, D (2011–21)
- **R. J. Umberger**, C (2008–14)
- **David Výborný**, RW (2000–08)
- **Zach Werenski**, D (2016–)

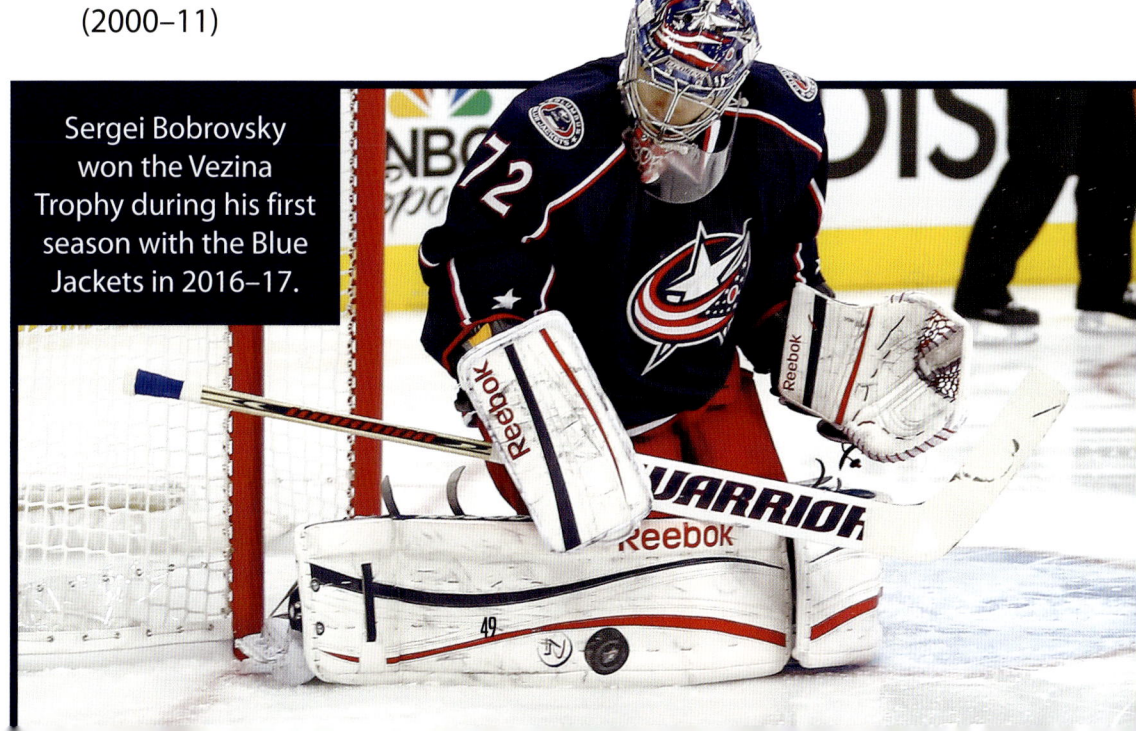

Sergei Bobrovsky won the Vezina Trophy during his first season with the Blue Jackets in 2016–17.

TEAM STATS AND RECORDS

ALL-TIME RECORD
- **Regular season:** 767–827–33–187
- **Postseason:** 15–26
- **Stanley Cup Final record:** 0–0

TOP COACHES
- **Todd Richards** (2011–16); 127–112–N/A–21 (regular season); 2–4 (postseason)
- **John Tortorella** (2016–21); 227–166–N/A–54 (regular season); 13–18 (postseason)

CAREER OFFENSIVE LEADERS
- **Games played:** Boone Jenner, 715
- **Goals:** Rick Nash, 289
- **Assists:** Rick Nash, 258
- **Points:** Rick Nash, 547
- **Penalty minutes:** Jared Boll, 1,195
- **Hat tricks:** Cam Atkinson, 6
- **Shorthanded goals:** Cam Atkinson, 16
- **Power play goals:** Rick Nash, 83
- **Game-winning goals:** Rick Nash, 44

CAREER GOALTENDING LEADERS
- **Games played:** Sergei Bobrovsky, 374
- **Wins:** Sergei Bobrovsky, 213
- **Goals against average:** Sergei Bobrovsky, 2.41
- **Save percentage:** Sergei Bobrovsky, .921
- **Shutouts:** Sergei Bobrovsky, 33

THE CANNON
All arenas are loud when the home team scores. But the atmosphere in Columbus is explosive. After each Blue Jackets goal, a replica cannon from the 1800s is fired. The cannon is a nod to the American Civil War (1861–65), which also inspired the Blue Jackets' nickname. Many of the blue coats worn by Union soldiers in the war were made in Columbus.

Right winger Josh Anderson controls the puck during Columbus's 2019 playoff series against the Lightning.

GREATEST SEASONS

The Columbus Blue Jackets were matched up against the Tampa Bay Lightning in the opening round of the 2018–19 Stanley Cup playoffs. Many experts predicted a short series. The Lightning had won the Presidents' Trophy, given to the team with the league's best regular-season record. They had tied a league record by winning 62 games.

No one gave Columbus a chance. It was a short series, but not the kind anyone predicted. The Blue Jackets beat Tampa Bay in four games. Columbus outscored the Lightning 19–8 in the sweep. It was the first time a Presidents' Trophy winner had ever been swept in the first round of the playoffs.

DALLAS STARS

TEAM HISTORY

The Dallas Stars were a product of the NHL's southern movement in the 1990s. The team began life as one of the six expansion teams added for the 1967–68 season. They played in Bloomington, Minnesota, and were called the North Stars. After 26 seasons that included two unsuccessful trips to the Stanley Cup Final, financial troubles drove the team to Dallas. There they dropped the *North* from their nickname and became the Stars.

Six years after arriving in Texas, a star-studded Dallas team reached the Final again. This time the Stars lifted the trophy after defeating the Buffalo Sabres. Though Dallas went back to the Final twice in the next 25 years, the team came up empty both times.

Center Neal Broten helped the Minnesota North Stars reach the Stanley Cup Final in both 1981 and 1991. He was still with the franchise when it moved to Dallas.

GREATEST PLAYERS

- **Ed Belfour**, G (1997–2002)
- **Brian Bellows**, LW (1982–92)
- **Jamie Benn**, LW (2009–)
- **Neal Broten**, C (1980–95)
- **Bill Goldsworthy**, RW (1967–76)
- **Jere Lehtinen**, RW (1995–2010)
- **Mike Modano**, C (1989–2010)
- **Brenden Morrow**, LW (1999–2013)
- **Tyler Seguin**, C (2013–)
- **Darryl Sydor**, D (1996–2003, 2006–07, 2008–09)
- **Marty Turco**, G (2001–10)
- **Sergei Zubov**, D (1996–2009)

After moving to Dallas, center Mike Modano's skilled play helped boost the popularity of hockey in Texas.

TEAM STATS AND RECORDS

ALL-TIME RECORD

- **Regular season:** 1987–1780–459–191
- **Postseason:** 208–203
- **Stanley Cup Final record:** 1–4

TOP COACHES

- **Ken Hitchcock** (1995–2002, 2017–18); 319–186–60–20 (regular season); 47–33 (postseason)
- **Dave Tippett** (2002–09); 271–156–28–37 (regular season); 21–26 (postseason)

CAREER OFFENSIVE LEADERS

- **Games played:** Mike Modano, 1,459
- **Goals:** Mike Modano, 557
- **Assists:** Mike Modano, 802
- **Points:** Mike Modano, 1,359
- **Penalty minutes:** Shane Churla, 1,883
- **Hat tricks:** Dino Ciccarelli, 14
- **Shorthanded goals:** Mike Modano, 29
- **Power play goals:** Mike Modano, 156
- **Game-winning goals:** Mike Modano, 92

CAREER GOALTENDING LEADERS

- **Games played:** Marty Turco, 509
- **Wins:** Marty Turco, 262
- **Goals against average:** Ed Belfour, 2.19
- **Save percentage:** Ben Bishop, .923
- **Shutouts:** Marty Turco, 40

GREATEST SEASONS

The 1998–99 Stars set franchise records of 51 wins and 114 points and reached the Stanley Cup Final. They faced off against the Buffalo Sabres. In a tense six-game series that featured four one-goal games, the Stars came out on top. The series will long be remembered for the controversial

Brett Hull's Stanley Cup–winning goal was highly controversial, especially among Sabres fans.

winning goal. In the third overtime of game 6, Dallas forward Brett Hull tapped in a rebound to win the Cup for the Stars. Buffalo fans and players were convinced Hull's left skate was in the crease when he scored, an illegal act that would have wiped out the goal. However, the play stood, and Dallas got its first title.

BILL MASTERTON

Bill Masterton was one of the original Minnesota North Stars. On January 13, 1968, the 29-year-old forward died after hitting his head on the ice during a home game. He was the first player to die from an injury in an NHL game. Masterton's death helped inspire more players to wear helmets, which eventually became a league-wide requirement. The league also created the Bill Masterton Memorial Trophy. The award is given each year to a player who demonstrates "perseverance, sportsmanship, and dedication to hockey."

DETROIT RED WINGS

TEAM HISTORY

Founded as the Detroit Cougars in 1926, the team was later known as the Falcons for two years before adopting the Red Wings nickname in 1932. The new name seemed to bring great success. Detroit won its first Stanley Cup in 1935–36 and another a year later.

Over the next two decades, the Red Wings added five more titles. Four of them came between 1949–50 and 1954–55. In that era, the team was led by the famous "Production Line" of center Sid Abel and wingers Gordie Howe and Ted Lindsay.

A long period of slow decline followed. By the early 1980s, critics mocked the team by calling them the "Dead Things." However, the drafting of future captain Steve Yzerman in 1983 sparked a gradual turnaround. The payoff came in 1996–97, when Detroit once again captured a title. The Red Wings added

Red Wings goaltender Terry Sawchuk was one of the greatest players of the Original Six era.

three more over the next 11 seasons and were once again considered one of the NHL's top franchises.

GREATEST PLAYERS

- **Sid Abel**, C (1938–43, 1945–52)
- **Pavel Datsyuk**, C (2001–16)
- **Alex Delvecchio**, C/LW (1951–73)
- **Sergei Fedorov**, C (1990–2003)
- **Gordie Howe**, RW (1946–71)
- **Red Kelly**, D/C (1947–60)
- **Niklas Kronwall**, D (2003–19)
- **Nicklas Lidström**, D (1991–2012)
- **Ted Lindsay**, LW (1944–57, 1964–65)
- **Chris Osgood**, G (1993–2001, 2005–11)
- **Terry Sawchuk**, G (1950–55, 1957–64, 1968–69)
- **Steve Yzerman**, C (1983–2006)
- **Henrik Zetterberg**, C (2002–18)

THE OCTOPUS

Detroit's 1952 Stanley Cup run gave birth to one of the NHL's most recognizable traditions. During game 3 of the Final against Montreal, a local fish market owner threw an octopus onto the ice. It was later claimed that the eight legs of the octopus represented the eight wins it then took to win the Stanley Cup. Though it now takes 16 victories to hoist the trophy, fans in Detroit have never stopped throwing the tentacled sea creatures onto the ice when the team is in the playoffs.

TEAM STATS AND RECORDS

ALL-TIME RECORD

- **Regular season**: 3097–2683–815–212
- **Postseason**: 325–296
- **Stanley Cup Final record**: 11–13

TOP COACHES

- **Tommy Ivan** (1947–54); 262–118–90–N/A (regular season); 36–31 (postseason)
- **Scotty Bowman** (1993–2002); 410–193–88–10 (regular season); 86–48 (postseason)

CAREER OFFENSIVE LEADERS

- **Games played**: Gordie Howe, 1,687
- **Goals**: Gordie Howe, 786
- **Assists**: Steve Yzerman, 1,063
- **Points**: Gordie Howe, 1,809
- **Penalty minutes**: Bob Probert, 2,090
- **Hat tricks**: Gordie Howe, 19
- **Shorthanded goals**: Steve Yzerman, 50
- **Power play goals**: Gordie Howe, 209
- **Game-winning goals**: Gordie Howe, 121

CAREER GOALTENDING LEADERS

- **Games played**: Terry Sawchuk, 734
- **Wins**: Terry Sawchuk, 350
- **Goals against average**: Dolly Dolson, 1.98
- **Save percentage**: Glenn Hall, .926
- **Shutouts**: Terry Sawchuk, 85

Center Steve Yzerman played his entire 22-year career for the Red Wings.

Before game 7 of the 2009 Stanley Cup Final, arena staff lowered an inflatable octopus to the ice. The octopus was a reference to the fan tradition of tossing these creatures onto the playing surface.

GREATEST SEASONS

In the NHL's Original Six era, a team needed to win eight playoff games to capture the Stanley Cup. No team had won the Cup without losing at least one game until the 1951–52 Red Wings steamrolled their competition. First, Detroit outscored the Toronto Maple Leafs 13–3 in a four-game semifinal sweep. Detroit goaltender Terry Sawchuk then allowed only two goals in four straight wins against Montreal in the Final. Sawchuk finished off the performance with back-to-back shutouts.

EDMONTON OILERS

Wayne Gretzky skates up the ice during his first season in the NHL.

TEAM HISTORY

The Edmonton Oilers began life in the WHA before moving to the NHL in 1979. The team arrived with a 19-year-old star named Wayne Gretzky already on the roster. He was on his way to becoming hockey's greatest scorer. Gretzky had plenty of help from future all-time greats including Mark Messier and Paul Coffey.

The Oilers established a high-scoring dynasty. Starting in 1983–84, the Oilers smashed several offensive records as they won four Stanley Cups in five years. Though Gretzky was traded after the 1987–88 title, Messier led the Oilers to a fifth Cup in 1989–90.

The Oilers then missed the playoffs for most of the next two decades. But hope arrived in 2015 with the addition of Connor McDavid. Like Gretzky before him, McDavid is considered the most talented player of his era. Edmonton fans hope he can lead the team back to glory.

GREATEST PLAYERS

- **Glenn Anderson**, RW (1980–91, 1996)
- **Paul Coffey**, D (1980–87)
- **Leon Draisaitl**, C (2014–)
- **Grant Fuhr**, G (1981–91)
- **Wayne Gretzky**, C (1979–88)
- **Jari Kurri**, RW (1980–90)
- **Kevin Lowe**, D (1979–92, 1996–98)
- **Connor McDavid**, C (2015–)
- **Mark Messier**, C (1979–91)
- **Ryan Nugent-Hopkins**, C (2011–)
- **Bill Ranford**, G (1988–96, 1999–2000)
- **Ryan Smyth**, LW (1995–2007, 2011–14)

At age 19, Connor McDavid was named the captain of the Oilers in 2016, making him the youngest permanent captain in NHL history.

EDMONTON OILERS

TEAM STATS AND RECORDS

ALL-TIME RECORD

- **Regular season:** 1617–1414–262–188
- **Postseason:** 189–136
- **Stanley Cup Final record:** 5–3

TOP COACHES

- **Glen Sather** (1979–89, 1993–94); 464–268–110–N/A (regular season); 89–37 (postseason)
- **Craig MacTavish** (2000–09); 301–252–47–56 (regular season); 19–17 (postseason)

CAREER OFFENSIVE LEADERS

- **Games played:** Kevin Lowe, 1,037
- **Goals:** Wayne Gretzky, 583
- **Assists:** Wayne Gretzky, 1,086
- **Points:** Wayne Gretzky, 1,669
- **Penalty minutes:** Kelly Buchberger, 1,747
- **Hat tricks:** Wayne Gretzky, 43
- **Shorthanded goals:** Wayne Gretzky, 55
- **Power play goals:** Leon Draisaitl, 146
- **Game-winning goals:** Glenn Anderson, 72

CAREER GOALTENDING LEADERS

- **Games played:** Bill Ranford, 449
- **Wins:** Grant Fuhr, 226
- **Goals against average:** Tommy Salo, 2.44
- **Save percentage:** Mike Smith, .913
- **Shutouts:** Tommy Salo, 23

GREATEST SEASONS

The Oilers scored goals at a rapid pace in the early 1980s. Entering the 1981–82 season, no NHL team had ever scored 400 goals in a single season. The Oilers broke that barrier five

The Oilers celebrate a goal against the New York Islanders in the 1984 Stanley Cup Final.

years in a row. Their high mark came in 1983–84 when the team piled up 446 goals and won a team-record 57 games. Edmonton then tallied 94 goals in 19 playoff games on its way to winning the team's first Stanley Cup title.

TAKING IT OUTDOORS

Outdoor NHL games are now a common sight, with multiple open-air contests taking place each year. But the idea was new in 2003 when the Oilers hosted the Heritage Classic. The game between Edmonton and the Montreal Canadiens was played in bitterly cold conditions at Edmonton's Commonwealth Stadium. Montreal won 4–3 as temperatures reached −22 degrees Fahrenheit (−30°C).

FLORIDA PANTHERS

Right winger Scott Mellanby scored the first goal in Florida Panthers franchise history.

TEAM HISTORY

The Panthers were founded as an expansion team in 1993. Within three years, they had reached the Stanley Cup Final. Florida lost in four games to the Colorado Avalanche in 1995–96, then endured two decades of mediocrity. Often, the biggest story surrounding the team was the low attendance at home games in sunny south Florida.

However, the Panthers emerged as an exciting force full of young talent in the 2020s. In 2022–23, Florida reached the Final again but lost to the Vegas Golden Knights. The next year, the Panthers finally broke through. They outlasted the Edmonton Oilers in a thrilling seven-game series to win their first title.

GREATEST PLAYERS

- **Aleksander Barkov**, C (2013–)
- **Sergei Bobrovsky**, G (2019–)
- **Pavel Bure**, RW (1999–02)
- **Aaron Ekblad**, D (2014–)
- **Jonathan Huberdeau**, LW (2012–22)
- **Olli Jokinen**, C (2000–08)
- **Roberto Luongo**, G (2000–06, 2014–19)
- **Scott Mellanby**, RW (1993–01)
- **Matthew Tkachuk**, LW (2022–)
- **John Vanbiesbrouck**, D (1993–98)
- **Tomáš Vokoun**, G (2007–11)
- **Stephen Weiss**, C (2002–13)

RAT TRICK

Before a game in October 1995, Panthers winger Scott Mellanby used a hockey stick to kill a rat that was scurrying through the team's home locker room. By the time the team reached the playoffs, fans who had heard the story were hurling plastic and rubber rats onto the ice after each Panthers goal. The practice continued through the team's run to the Stanley Cup Final. After the season, the league banned the celebration.

TEAM STATS AND RECORDS

ALL-TIME RECORD
- **Regular season:** 1041–944–142–228
- **Postseason:** 54–55
- **Stanley Cup Final record:** 1–2

TOP COACHES
- **Doug MacLean** (1995–98); 83–71–33–N/A (regular season); 13–14 (postseason)
- **Paul Maurice** (2022–); 94–56–N/A–14 (regular season); 29–16 (postseason)

CAREER OFFENSIVE LEADERS
- **Games played:** Aleksander Barkov, 737
- **Goals:** Aleksander Barkov, 266
- **Assists:** Aleksander Barkov, 445
- **Points:** Aleksander Barkov, 711
- **Penalty minutes:** Paul Laus, 1,702
- **Hat tricks:** Pavel Bure, 10
- **Shorthanded goals:** Radek Dvořák, 16
- **Power play goals:** Aleksander Barkov, 75
- **Game-winning goals:** Aleksander Barkov, 48

CAREER GOALTENDING LEADERS
- **Games played:** Roberto Luongo, 572
- **Wins:** Roberto Luongo, 230
- **Goals against average:** Tomáš Vokoun, 2.57
- **Save percentage:** Tomáš Vokoun, .923
- **Shutouts:** Roberto Luongo, 38

In 2023, Matthew Tkachuk was a finalist for the Hart Memorial Trophy, the NHL's most valuable player award.

Florida center Sam Reinhart celebrates after scoring the go-ahead goal in game 7 of the 2024 Stanley Cup Final.

GREATEST SEASONS

After winning only 53 games in their first two seasons combined, the Panthers shocked the hockey world by winning 41 in 1995–96. But the surprises didn't end there. Florida stunned the favored Boston Bruins, Philadelphia Flyers, and Pittsburgh Penguins on a thrilling run to the Stanley Cup Final.

In 2023–24, the Panthers finally came out on top. However, the road to a championship wasn't easy. Facing the Edmonton Oilers in the Final, the Panthers won the first three games. Edmonton then charged back and won the next three, setting up a tense seventh game in Florida. Panthers forward Sam Reinhart broke a 1–1 tie with 3:49 left in the second period. The goal held up as the winner to deliver the Panthers their first Stanley Cup.

LOS ANGELES KINGS

Los Angeles Kings goaltender Wayne Rutledge makes a save during the team's first season in 1967.

TEAM HISTORY

The Los Angeles Kings were one of two NHL expansion teams placed in California in 1967. But the other, the Oakland Seals/California Golden Seals, had packed up and left for Cleveland by the late 1970s. Alone on the West Coast, the Kings were mostly ignored by the hockey world. That all changed in August 1988, when owner Bruce McNall made a bold trade to bring superstar Wayne Gretzky to Los Angeles.

Gretzky delivered star power, but the Kings failed to capture a Stanley Cup in his seven years with the team. For that, Kings fans had to wait until the 2011–12 season. The Kings added a second title two years later but then struggled to find playoff success again in the years that followed.

GREATEST PLAYERS

- **Rob Blake**, D (1990–2001, 2006–08)
- **Dustin Brown**, RW (2003–22)
- **Marcel Dionne**, C (1975–87)
- **Drew Doughty**, D (2008–)
- **Wayne Gretzky**, C (1988–96)
- **Anže Kopitar**, C (2006–)
- **Bernie Nicholls**, C (1981–90)
- **Mattias Norström**, C (1996–2007)
- **Jonathan Quick**, G (2007–23)
- **Luc Robitaille**, LW (1986–94, 1997–2001, 2003–06)
- **Dave Taylor**, RW (1977–94)
- **Rogie Vachon**, G (1971–78)

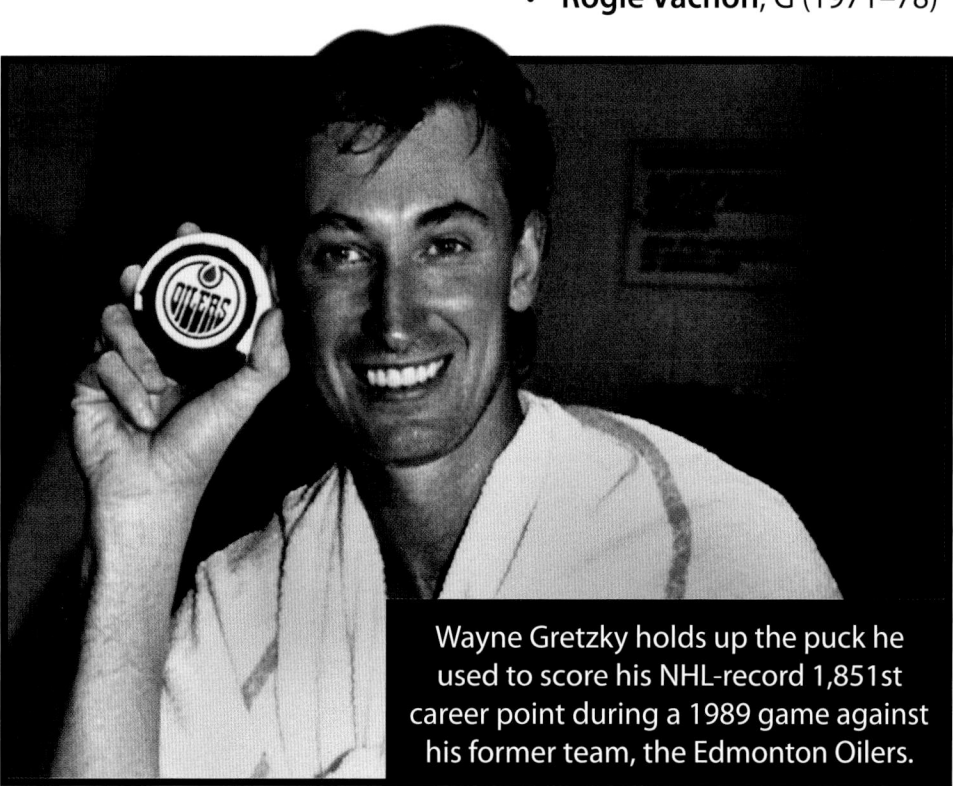

Wayne Gretzky holds up the puck he used to score his NHL-record 1,851st career point during a 1989 game against his former team, the Edmonton Oilers.

TEAM STATS AND RECORDS

ALL-TIME RECORD
- **Regular season:** 1889–1907–424–198
- **Postseason:** 117–156
- **Stanley Cup Final record:** 2–1

TOP COACHES
- **Andy Murray** (1999–2006); 215–175–58–32 (regular season); 10–14 (postseason)
- **Darryl Sutter** (2011–17); 225–147–N/A–53 (regular season); 42–27 (postseason)

CAREER OFFENSIVE LEADERS
- **Games played:** Anže Kopitar, 1,373
- **Goals:** Luc Robitaille, 557
- **Assists:** Anže Kopitar, 792
- **Points:** Marcel Dionne, 1,307
- **Penalty minutes:** Marty McSorley, 1846
- **Hat tricks:** Marcel Dionne, 24
- **Shorthanded goals:** Bernie Nicholls, 25
- **Power play goals:** Luc Robitaille, 210
- **Game-winning goals:** Luc Robitaille, 73

CAREER GOALTENDING LEADERS
- **Games played:** Jonathan Quick, 743
- **Wins:** Jonathan Quick, 370
- **Goals against average:** Félix Potvin, 2.35
- **Save percentage:** Jonathan Quick, .911
- **Shutouts:** Jonathan Quick, 57

GREATEST SEASONS

The early 2011–12 season didn't look memorable for Kings fans. The team fired head coach Terry Murray after a poor start. However, his replacement, Darryl Sutter, inspired Los Angeles to the playoffs. There the Kings upset three higher-seeded

Talented defenseman Drew Doughty helped the Kings win the Stanley Cup in 2012 and 2014.

teams on their way to the Final. A six-game series win over the New Jersey Devils finished off the improbable title run.

Two years later, the Kings found themselves down 3–0 to the San Jose Sharks in the first round. Los Angeles rallied and won the series. After winning two more seven-game series to reach the Final, the Kings knocked off the New York Rangers to win the Stanley Cup again. Defenseman Alec Martinez's overtime goal in game 5 sealed the championship.

THE MIRACLE ON MANCHESTER

On April 10, 1982, the Kings were trailing the Edmonton Oilers 5–0 heading into the third period of game 3 in the teams' playoff series. Miraculously, the Kings rallied to tie the game. Rookie Daryl Evans then scored 2:35 into overtime for a 6–5 win. The game was called the "Miracle on Manchester" after the arena's address. Forty years later it was still the largest comeback ever in a playoff game.

MINNESOTA WILD

TEAM HISTORY

When the North Stars left for Dallas in 1993, hockey-loving Minnesotans were eager to get an NHL team again. They did not have to wait long. The Wild were announced as an expansion team in 1997 and began play in 2000. The team was popular from the start.

Minnesota sold out its home arena for 409 straight games. The streak did not end until 2010. Fans didn't always see winning hockey, however. Though the Wild made a surprise run to the Western Conference finals in their third season, the team won only four total playoff series in its first 13 appearances through 2023.

Goaltender Manny Fernandez helped the Wild reach the Western Conference finals in 2003.

GREATEST PLAYERS

- **Niklas Bäckström**, G (2006–15)
- **Jonas Brodin**, D (2012–)
- **Andrew Brunette**, LW (2001–04, 2008–11)
- **Devan Dubnyk**, G (2015–20)
- **Marián Gáborík**, RW (2000–09)
- **Kirill Kaprizov**, LW (2020–)
- **Mikko Koivu**, C (2005–20)
- **Zach Parise**, LW (2012–21)
- **Nick Schultz**, D (2001–12)
- **Jared Spurgeon**, D (2010–)
- **Ryan Suter**, D (2012–21)
- **Wes Walz**, C (2000–07)

Zach Parise was one of many Wild players who were born in Minnesota.

TEAM STATS AND RECORDS

ALL-TIME RECORD
- **Regular season:** 897–680–55–181
- **Postseason:** 34–62
- **Stanley Cup Final record:** 0–0

TOP COACHES
- **Jacques Lemaire** (2000–09); 293–255–55–53 (regular season); 11–18 (postseason)
- **Dean Evason** (2020–23); 147–77–N/A–27 (regular season); 8–15 (postseason)

CAREER OFFENSIVE LEADERS
- **Games played:** Mikko Koivu, 1,028
- **Goals:** Marián Gáborík, 219
- **Assists:** Mikko Koivu, 504
- **Points:** Mikko Koivu, 709
- **Penalty minutes:** Matt Johnson, 698
- **Hat tricks:** Marián Gáborík, 9
- **Shorthanded goals:** Wes Walz, 14
- **Power play goals:** Zach Parise, 69
- **Game-winning goals:** Marián Gáborík, 43

CAREER GOALTENDING LEADERS
- **Games played:** Niklas Bäckström, 409
- **Wins:** Niklas Bäckström, 194
- **Goals against average:** Dwayne Roloson, 2.28
- **Save percentage:** Dwayne Roloson, .919
- **Shutouts:** Niklas Bäckström, 28

HOMETOWN TALENT

The state of Minnesota has produced more than 300 NHL players. That is the most of any US state. Through the Wild's first 23 seasons, 34 players who were born in Minnesota have suited up for the team.

GREATEST SEASONS

The Wild weren't expected to go far in the 2002–03 playoffs. In the first round they quickly fell behind the favored Colorado Avalanche 3–1. But Minnesota rallied to win the series, taking both game 6 and game 7 in overtime.

Next up were the Vancouver Canucks. Again, Minnesota fell behind 3–1 before rallying to win the series. The Wild's run ended in the Western Conference finals, but they had already made history. No NHL team had ever won two series in the same playoff year when trailing 3–1.

> Slovak right winger Marián Gáborík was a star for the Wild in the team's first decade.

MONTREAL CANADIENS

Henri Richard holds the Stanley Cup after the Canadiens' 1966 victory. The team has won the championship an incredible 23 times.

TEAM HISTORY

No team has dominated the NHL for long stretches of time like the Montreal Canadiens. The most successful franchise in league history won at least one Stanley Cup in every decade from the 1910s to the 1990s. That includes a stretch of five straight championships in the late 1950s and early 1960s along with four straight in the late 1970s.

Though the Canadiens have not fared as well recently, the team remains a point of pride for French-speaking Canadians. The team is known as *Les Habitants*, a name for early French settlers in Quebec. They are called the Habs for short. They are revered in Quebec, and playing for the team is both an honor and a pressure-packed experience for natives of the province.

GREATEST PLAYERS

- **Jean Béliveau**, C (1950–51, 1952–71)
- **Yvan Cournoyer**, RW (1963–78)
- **Ken Dryden**, G (1971–73, 1974–79)
- **Bernie Geoffrion**, RW (1950–64)
- **Doug Harvey**, D (1947–61)
- **Guy Lafleur**, RW (1971–85)
- **Howie Morenz**, C (1923–34, 1936–37)
- **Jacques Plante**, G (1952, 1954–63)
- **Henri Richard**, C (1955–75)
- **Maurice Richard**, RW (1942–60)
- **Larry Robinson**, D (1972–89)
- **Serge Savard**, D (1967–81)

Right winger Guy Lafleur won five Stanley Cup championships with the Canadiens in the 1970s.

TEAM STATS AND RECORDS

ALL-TIME RECORD
- **Regular season:** 3556–2432–837–208
- **Postseason:** 440–321
- **Stanley Cup Final record:** 23–10

TOP COACHES
- **Toe Blake** (1955–68); 500–155–159–N/A (regular season); 82–37 (postseason)
- **Scotty Bowman** (1971–79); 419–110–105–N/A (regular season); 70–28 (postseason)

CAREER OFFENSIVE LEADERS
- **Games played:** Henri Richard, 1,258
- **Goals:** Maurice Richard, 544
- **Assists:** Guy Lafleur, 728
- **Points:** Guy Lafleur, 1,246
- **Penalty minutes:** Chris Nilan, 2,248
- **Hat tricks:** Maurice Richard, 26
- **Shorthanded goals:** Guy Carbonneau, 28
- **Power play goals:** Jean Béliveau, 173
- **Game-winning goals:** Guy Lafleur, 94

CAREER GOALTENDING LEADERS
- **Games played:** Carey Price, 712
- **Wins:** Carey Price, 361
- **Goals against average:** George Hainsworth, 1.78
- **Save percentage:** Ken Dryden, .922
- **Shutouts:** George Hainsworth, 75

GREATEST SEASONS

While Montreal has had several of the greatest teams in NHL history, the 1976–77 team is often considered the best ever to take the ice. The Canadiens featured nine future Hall of Fame players that season. Montreal lost only eight games all

Serge Savard, *left*, was a member of seven Canadiens championship teams, including the legendary 1976–77 group.

year and set an NHL record with 132 points in the standings. The Canadiens outscored their opponents by 216 goals, also an NHL record. It all ended with a four-game sweep of the Boston Bruins in the Stanley Cup Final. Forward Jacques Lemaire scored both goals in the clinching game, including the overtime winner.

A DIVIDED CITY

Montreal has large populations of both French and English speakers. In the NHL's early days, the Canadiens represented the French population. The Montreal Wanderers were the English team in 1917 but did not finish the season. They were later replaced by the Montreal Maroons, who played to mostly English fans from 1924 until the team folded in 1938. Though their French Canadian heritage makes the Canadiens immensely proud, they are now passionately followed by fans of all backgrounds.

NASHVILLE PREDATORS

Finnish defenseman Kimmo Timonen was an original member of the Predators.

TEAM HISTORY

Nashville originally built its hockey arena in the mid-1990s to bring the New Jersey Devils to Tennessee. But when that plan didn't work, NHL commissioner Gary Bettman delivered a brand-new team to the state instead. It took the Predators a long time to become successful. But the team took a patient approach. The Predators' original general manager, David

Poile, served in that role from 1997 to 2023. Nashville's original head coach, Barry Trotz, was with the team for 15 seasons. That consistency paid off, as the team reached the playoffs 15 times in 18 seasons between 2003–04 and 2021–22.

Games in Nashville are among the biggest parties in the league. The team's arena sits on Broadway, a street famed for live music. It's not uncommon to see rock and country acts inside the arena as well.

GREATEST PLAYERS

- **Ryan Ellis**, D (2011–21)
- **Martin Erat**, RW (2001–13)
- **Filip Forsberg**, C (2013–)
- **Ryan Johansen**, C (2016–23)
- **Roman Josi**, D (2011–)
- **David Legwand**, C (1999–2014)
- **Pekka Rinne**, G (2005–06, 2008–21)
- **Juuse Saros**, G (2015–)
- **Craig Smith**, C (2011–20)
- **Kimmo Timonen**, D (1998–2007)
- **Tomáš Vokoun**, G (1998–2007)
- **Shea Weber**, D (2006–16)

SHOWING THEIR TEETH

The Predators' logo features a saber-toothed cat. Construction workers found fossilized bones of the extinct animal when digging the foundation for a Nashville skyscraper in the early 1970s. When it came time to name the city's NHL team, the logo fit. Fans named the team the Predators to match with the design.

TEAM STATS AND RECORDS

ALL-TIME RECORD
- **Regular season:** 986–748–60–183
- **Postseason:** 56–75
- **Stanley Cup Final record:** 0–1

TOP COACHES
- **Barry Trotz** (1998–2014); 557–479–60–100 (regular season); 19–31 (postseason)
- **Peter Laviolette** (2014–20); 248–143–N/A–60 (regular season); 32–29 (postseason)

CAREER OFFENSIVE LEADERS
- **Games played:** David Legwand, 956
- **Goals:** Filip Forsberg, 287
- **Assists:** Roman Josi, 505
- **Points:** Roman Josi, 686
- **Penalty minutes:** Jordin Tootoo, 725
- **Hat tricks:** Filip Forsberg, 10
- **Shorthanded goals:** Greg Johnson, 11
- **Power play goals:** Shea Weber, 80
- **Game-winning goals:** Filip Forsberg, 54

CAREER GOALTENDING LEADERS
- **Games played:** Pekka Rinne, 683
- **Wins:** Pekka Rinne, 369
- **Goals against average:** Pekka Rinne, 2.43
- **Save percentage:** Pekka Rinne/Juuse Saros, .917
- **Shutouts:** Pekka Rinne, 60

GREATEST SEASONS

The Predators weren't expected to make too much noise in the 2016–17 playoffs after sneaking in as one of two wild card teams in the Western Conference. But Nashville shocked the top-seeded Chicago Blackhawks in a first-round sweep. After knocking out the St. Louis Blues and Anaheim Ducks, the Predators faced the Pittsburgh Penguins in the Stanley

Goaltender Pekka Rinne makes a save during the Predators' 2016–17 playoff run.

Cup Final. Nashville lost the first two games, then won game 3 and game 4 at home. However, the Predators were shut out in games 5 and 6 to fall short of a championship.

Shea Weber, 6, and his teammates battle for the puck against the San Jose Sharks during the 2016 playoffs.

NEW JERSEY DEVILS

TEAM HISTORY

For the first decade of their history, the New Jersey Devils were a team on the move. The franchise was founded as the Kansas City Scouts in 1974. After two failed years in the Midwest, the Scouts moved to Denver and became the Colorado Rockies. When that didn't work, shipbuilder John McMullen moved the franchise to New Jersey in 1982.

Wherever it was, the team was rough to watch. The team didn't win 30 games in a season until 1987–88.

Defenseman Ken Daneyko played 20 seasons with the New Jersey Devils, and fans have nicknamed him "Mr. Devil."

Wayne Gretzky once insulted the Devils by calling the team a "Mickey Mouse operation." But when the Devils hired general manager Lou Lamoriello before that 1987–88 season, their fortune started to change. Lamoriello's wise moves eventually earned the team its first Stanley Cup in 1995. Two more titles followed in the next decade.

GREATEST PLAYERS

- **Martin Brodeur**, G (1991–92, 1993–2014)
- **Ken Daneyko**, D (1983, 1985–2003)
- **Patrik Eliáš**, LW (1995–2016)
- **Scott Gomez**, C (1999–2007, 2014–15)
- **Bobby Holík**, C (1992–2002, 2008–09)
- **John MacLean**, RW (1983–97)
- **Kirk Muller**, LW (1984–91)
- **Scott Niedermayer**, D (1991–2004)
- **Zach Parise**, LW (2005–12)
- **Scott Stevens**, D (1991–2004)
- **Petr Sýkora**, RW (1995–2002, 2011–12)
- **Travis Zajac**, C (2006–21)

A DAY WITH THE CUP

When the Devils won the Stanley Cup in 1995, the team started a tradition that spread across the NHL. Each player was given 24 hours with the trophy to take it wherever they wanted. Over the years, players on various teams have taken the Cup up mountains or to faraway countries. Others have eaten cereal out of its bowl or even baptized their children in it.

TEAM STATS AND RECORDS

ALL-TIME RECORD
- **Regular season:** 1651–1709–328–191
- **Postseason:** 142–129
- **Stanley Cup Final record:** 3–2

TOP COACHES
- **Jacques Lemaire** (1993–98, 2009–11); 276–166–57–10 (regular season); 35–26 (postseason)
- **Pat Burns** (2002–04); 89–45–22–8 (regular season); 17–12 (postseason)

CAREER OFFENSIVE LEADERS
- **Games played:** Ken Daneyko, 1,283
- **Goals:** Patrik Eliáš, 408
- **Assists:** Patrik Eliáš, 617
- **Points:** Patrik Eliáš, 1,025
- **Penalty minutes:** Ken Daneyko, 2,516
- **Hat tricks:** Patrik Eliáš, 8
- **Shorthanded goals:** John Madden, 17
- **Power play goals:** Patrik Eliáš, 113
- **Game-winning goals:** Patrik Eliáš, 80

CAREER GOALTENDING LEADERS
- **Games played:** Martin Brodeur, 1,259
- **Wins:** Martin Brodeur, 688
- **Goals against average:** Martin Brodeur, 2.24
- **Save percentage:** Cory Schneider, .915
- **Shutouts:** Martin Brodeur, 124

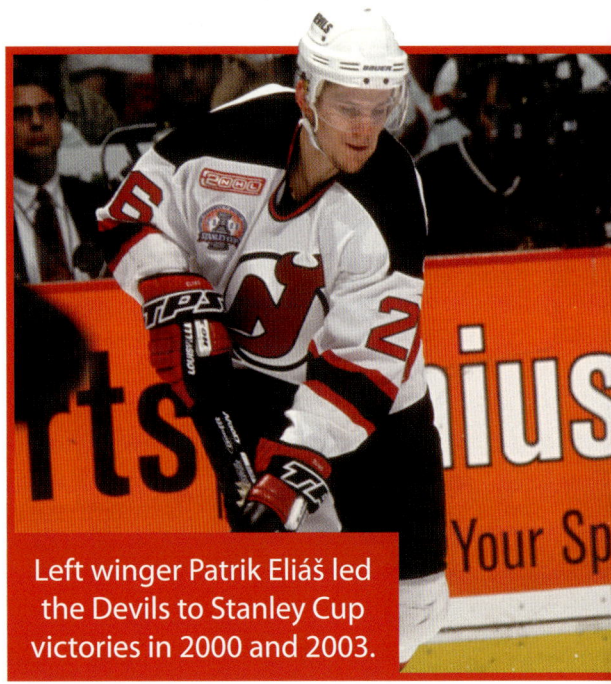

Left winger Patrik Eliáš led the Devils to Stanley Cup victories in 2000 and 2003.

Legendary goaltender Martin Brodeur celebrates after winning the Stanley Cup in 1995.

GREATEST SEASONS

The Devils finished the lockout-shortened 1994–95 season with a modest record of only 22–18–8. But the team turned into a powerhouse in the playoffs. The Devils lost only four games on their way to a championship. That included a four-game sweep over the heavily favored Detroit Red Wings in the Final.

Five years later, the Devils rallied from 3–1 down against the Philadelphia Flyers to win the Eastern Conference finals in seven games. They then played the Dallas Stars in the Final. Jason Arnott's goal in double overtime of game 6 won New Jersey its second Cup.

NEW YORK ISLANDERS

TEAM HISTORY

The Islanders were formed in 1972 at the height of the NHL's battle with the WHA. The team was allowed into the NHL to make sure the WHA wouldn't put a team in New York. After two rough seasons in which the Isles won only 31 combined games, the team started to improve. Under the watchful eye of legendary head coach Al Arbour, New York built a powerful team by the end of the decade.

In 1979–80, it started a run of four straight Stanley Cup victories. In those four Stanley Cup Finals, the team had an overall record of 16–3. Their time at the top ended in 1983–84 when they lost to the Edmonton Oilers in the Final. Islanders fans have been mostly disappointed in the four decades since. The team has not come anywhere close to that earlier level of success.

Right winger Mike Bossy had a career-high 69 goals while playing for the Islanders in 1978–79.

GREATEST PLAYERS

- **Josh Bailey**, C (2008–23)
- **Mike Bossy**, RW (1977–87)
- **Clark Gillies**, LW (1974–86)
- **Butch Goring**, C (1980–84)
- **Pat LaFontaine**, C (1984–91)
- **Bob Nystrom**, RW (1972–86)
- **Denis Potvin**, D (1973–88)
- **Billy Smith**, G (1972–89)
- **Brent Sutter**, C (1981–91)
- **John Tavares**, C (2009–18)
- **John Tonelli**, LW (1978–86)
- **Bryan Trottier**, C (1975–90)

Josh Bailey played his 1,000th game with the Islanders in 2022, becoming the third player in franchise history to reach that mark.

THE EASTER EPIC

On Saturday, April 18, 1987, the Islanders squared off with the Washington Capitals. It was the longest game 7 in NHL playoff history. Despite a combined 125 shots on goal, the game stayed tied 2–2 until the 8:47 mark of the fourth overtime. New York winger Pat LaFontaine finally scored the winning goal at 1:58 a.m. By then it was Easter Sunday, and the game was dubbed the "Easter Epic."

TEAM STATS AND RECORDS

ALL-TIME RECORD

- **Regular season:** 1806–1680–347–201
- **Postseason:** 175–149
- **Stanley Cup Final record:** 4–1

TOP COACHES

- **Al Arbour** (1973–94, 2008); 740–537–223–N/A (regular season); 119–79 (postseason)
- **Jack Capuano** (2011–17); 227–192–N/A–64 (regular season); 10–14 (postseason)

CAREER OFFENSIVE LEADERS

- **Games played:** Bryan Trottier, 1,123
- **Goals:** Mike Bossy, 573
- **Assists:** Bryan Trottier, 853
- **Points:** Bryan Trottier, 1,353
- **Penalty minutes:** Mick Vukota, 1,879
- **Hat tricks:** Mike Bossy, 39
- **Shorthanded goals:** Anders Kallur, 19
- **Power play goals:** Mike Bossy, 180
- **Game-winning goals:** Mike Bossy, 80

CAREER GOALTENDING LEADERS

- **Games played:** Billy Smith, 674
- **Wins:** Billy Smith, 304
- **Goals against average:** Ilya Sorokin, 2.54
- **Save percentage:** Ilya Sorokin, .919
- **Shutouts:** Glenn Resch, 25

GREATEST SEASONS

The Islanders' first Stanley Cup victory in 1980 ended in dramatic fashion. Winger Bob Nystrom tipped home a pass from linemate John Tonelli to defeat the Philadelphia Flyers in game 6 of the Final. He clinched New York's first title. Two years later, the Islanders set team records of 54 wins and 118 points.

Captain Denis Potvin, 5, reaches out to touch the Stanley Cup following the team's 1980 championship victory.

That dominance was on display through the playoffs as well. New York swept both the Quebec Nordiques in the Eastern Conference finals and the Vancouver Canucks in the Stanley Cup Final.

NEW YORK RANGERS

Coach Lester Patrick, *top row, fourth from left*, led the Rangers to Stanley Cup victories in 1928 and 1940.

TEAM HISTORY

The New York Rangers were founded in 1926 by Tex Rickard, the owner of the team's famous Madison Square Garden arena. When sportswriters started calling Rickard's team "Tex's Rangers," the nickname stuck. And the Rangers stuck near the top of the standings for many of their early seasons. By 1940, New York had won three Stanley Cups.

However, the Rangers struggled to keep up in the Original Six era. In that 25-year stretch, New York missed the playoffs 18 times. The Rangers did not win another Stanley Cup until 1994, famously ending their brutal 54-year championship drought.

GREATEST PLAYERS

- **Andy Bathgate**, RW (1952–64)
- **Ed Giacomin**, G (1965–75)
- **Rod Gilbert**, RW (1960, 1962–77)
- **Vic Hadfield**, LW (1961–74)
- **Harry Howell**, D (1952–69)
- **Chris Kreider**, LW (2013–)
- **Brian Leetch**, D (1988–2004)
- **Henrik Lundqvist**, G (2005–20)
- **Mark Messier**, C (1991–97, 2000–04)
- **Jean Ratelle**, C (1961–75)
- **Mike Richter**, G (1989–2002)
- **Walt Tkaczuk**, C (1968–81)

Center Mark Messier scores against goaltender Martin Brodeur of the New Jersey Devils in game 6 of the 1994 Eastern Conference finals.

TEAM STATS AND RECORDS

ALL-TIME RECORD
- **Regular season:** 3037–2785–808–176
- **Postseason:** 267–286
- **Stanley Cup Final record:** 4–7

TOP COACHES
- **Lester Patrick** (1926–39); 281–216–107–N/A (regular season); 32–26–7 (postseason)
- **Emile Francis** (1965–75); 342–209–103–N/A (regular season); 34–41 (postseason)

CAREER OFFENSIVE LEADERS
- **Games played:** Harry Howell, 1,160
- **Goals:** Rod Gilbert, 406
- **Assists:** Brian Leetch, 741
- **Points:** Rod Gilbert, 1,021
- **Penalty minutes:** Ron Greschner, 1,226
- **Hat tricks:** Bill Cook, 9
- **Shorthanded goals:** Mark Messier, 23
- **Power play goals:** Camille Henry, 116
- **Game-winning goals:** Rod Gilbert, 52

CAREER GOALTENDING LEADERS
- **Games played:** Henrik Lundqvist, 887
- **Wins:** Henrik Lundqvist, 459
- **Goals against average:** Lorne Chabot, 1.63
- **Save percentage:** Igor Shesterkin, .921
- **Shutouts:** Henrik Lundqvist, 64

MESSIER'S GUARANTEE

The Rangers trailed the New Jersey Devils 3–2 before game 6 of the 1994 Eastern Conference finals. New York captain Mark Messier told reporters before the game that he could guarantee a win. Messier then backed up his bold talk by scoring a hat trick as the Rangers won 4–2 to force game 7.

The Rangers reached the second round of the playoffs in 2017, beating the Montreal Canadiens in the first round before losing to the Ottawa Senators.

GREATEST SEASONS

The Rangers won 52 games and captured the Atlantic Division title in 1993–94. This marked the fifth time the team had finished the regular season in first place. But the Rangers were far from done.

After romping over the New York Islanders and Washington Capitals in the first two rounds of the playoffs, New York faced two tough tests. Winger Stéphane Matteau's game 7 double overtime winner knocked out the rival New Jersey Devils in the Eastern Conference finals. The Rangers then needed all seven games in the Stanley Cup Final to defeat the Vancouver Canucks and claim New York's first Stanley Cup since 1940.

OTTAWA SENATORS

TEAM HISTORY

A team known as the Ottawa Senators was one of the founding members of the NHL in 1917. But that version folded in 1934. After a nearly 60-year wait, the league returned to Canada's capital.

The new Senators began play in 1992–93, but success took a little longer. The club won only 33 games in its first three seasons combined. However, new coach Jacques Martin helped start a turnaround in 1995–96. The next year, the Senators began a run of 11 straight appearances

Alexei Yashin was the Senators' top scorer for several seasons in the mid-1990s.

in the playoffs. Bryan Murray had replaced Martin by the time the Senators reached their only Stanley Cup Final in 2006–07.

In the years since, Ottawa has struggled to keep up with the rest of the league. Near the end of the 2023–24 season, Martin was brought back as head coach. Still, the team missed the playoffs for the seventh straight season.

GREATEST PLAYERS

- **Daniel Alfredsson**, RW (1995–2013)
- **Craig Anderson**, G (2011–20)
- **Radek Bonk**, C (1995–2004)
- **Mike Fisher**, C (1999–2011)
- **Erik Karlsson**, D (2009–18)
- **Patrick Lalime**, G (1999–2004)
- **Chris Neil**, RW (2001–17)
- **Chris Phillips**, D (1997–2015)
- **Wade Redden**, D (1996–2008)
- **Jason Spezza**, C (2002–14)
- **Brady Tkachuk**, LW (2018–)
- **Alexei Yashin**, C (1993–2001)

Right winger Daniel Alfredsson won the Calder Memorial Trophy after his rookie year with Ottawa in 1995–96.

OTTAWA SENATORS

TEAM STATS AND RECORDS

ALL-TIME RECORD
- **Regular season**: 1080–1058–115–188
- **Postseason**: 72–79
- **Stanley Cup Final record**: 0–1

TOP COACHES
- **Jacques Martin** (1995–2004, 2023–); 367–261–96–24 (regular season); 31–38 (postseason)
- **Bryan Murray** (2005–07); 107–55–0–20 (regular season); 18–16 (postseason)

CAREER OFFENSIVE LEADERS
- **Games played**: Chris Phillips, 1,179
- **Goals**: Daniel Alfredsson, 426
- **Assists**: Daniel Alfredsson, 682
- **Points**: Daniel Alfredsson, 1,108
- **Penalty minutes**: Chris Neil, 2,522
- **Hat tricks**: Daniel Alfredsson, 8
- **Shorthanded goals**: Daniel Alfredsson, 25
- **Power play goals**: Daniel Alfredsson, 131
- **Game-winning goals**: Daniel Alfredsson, 69

CAREER GOALTENDING LEADERS
- **Games played**: Craig Anderson, 435
- **Wins**: Craig Anderson, 202
- **Goals against average**: Patrick Lalime/Ron Tugnutt, 2.32
- **Save percentage**: Craig Anderson/Robin Lehner, .914
- **Shutouts**: Patrick Lalime, 30

The modern Senators reached their first Stanley Cup Final in 2007, but they lost to the Anaheim Ducks.

GREATEST SEASONS

The Senators had been in the playoffs for ten straight years by the time the 2006–07 playoffs rolled around. But the closest they had come to the Stanley Cup was a heartbreaking seven-game loss in the 2002–03 Eastern Conference finals. In spring 2007, however, the Senators won three straight series in the Eastern Conference.

The conference finals ended in dramatic fashion. Star Senators winger Daniel Alfredsson scored 9:32 into overtime of game 5 to send Ottawa to the Stanley Cup Final. The team's luck ran out there, however. The Senators lost three one-goal games to the Anaheim Ducks on the way to a 4–1 series defeat.

A HISTORY OF WINNING

Though the modern version of the Ottawa Senators has struggled, 11 Stanley Cup banners still hang from the rafters at the team's home arena. The original Ottawa Senators won four Stanley Cups in the 1920s. The team also won three Cups under the Senators name before the NHL was created. The other four banners are for the Ottawa Silver Seven, who won the Cup four times in the 1900s.

PHILADELPHIA FLYERS

The Flyers' physical style of play brought them major success in the 1970s.

TEAM HISTORY

The Philadelphia Flyers were the first of the 1967 expansion teams to win the Stanley Cup. But it was how the team did it that established Philadelphia's hockey identity. Fighting had always been part of the NHL, but the Flyers took it to a new level in the 1970s. The team's brand-new arena sat on South Broad Street. After roughing up the league with hard hits and brawls, the Flyers became known as the "Broad Street Bullies."

Critics called the Flyers a dirty team. But the Flyers were skilled and won back-to-back Cups in 1973–74 and 1974–75. In the 50 years since that run, the Flyers made six more Stanley Cup Final appearances. But the team came up short each time.

GREATEST PLAYERS

- **Bill Barber**, LW (1972–84)
- **Bobby Clarke**, C (1969–84)
- **Sean Couturier**, C (2011–)
- **Claude Giroux**, C/LW (2008–22)
- **Ron Hextall**, G (1986–92, 1994–99)
- **Mark Howe**, D (1982–92)
- **Tim Kerr**, C/RW (1980–91)
- **John LeClair**, LW (1995–2004)
- **Eric Lindros**, C (1992–2000)
- **Rick MacLeish**, C (1970–81, 1984)
- **Bernie Parent**, G (1967–71, 1973–79)
- **Brian Propp**, LW (1979–90)

Flyers center Sean Couturier handles the puck during an outdoor game against the New Jersey Devils in 2024.

PHILADELPHIA FLYERS

TEAM STATS AND RECORDS

ALL-TIME RECORD
- **Regular season:** 2173–1569–457–218
- **Postseason:** 231–218
- **Stanley Cup Final record:** 2–6

TOP COACHES
- **Fred Shero** (1971–78); 308–151–95–N/A (regular season); 48–35 (postseason)
- **Mike Keenan** (1984–88); 190–102–28–N/A (regular season); 32–25 (postseason)

CAREER OFFENSIVE LEADERS
- **Games played:** Bobby Clarke, 1,144
- **Goals:** Bill Barber, 420
- **Assists:** Bobby Clarke, 852
- **Points:** Bobby Clarke, 1,210
- **Penalty minutes:** Rick Tocchet, 1,815
- **Hat tricks:** Tim Kerr, 17
- **Shorthanded goals:** Bobby Clarke, 32
- **Power play goals:** Tim Kerr, 144
- **Game-winning goals:** John LeClair, 61

CAREER GOALTENDING LEADERS
- **Games played:** Ron Hextall, 489
- **Wins:** Ron Hextall, 240
- **Goals against average:** Roman Čechmánek, 1.96
- **Save percentage:** Roman Čechmánek, .923
- **Shutouts:** Bernie Parent, 50

GRITTY

The Flyers introduced a new mascot before the 2018–19 season. Gritty became an instant hit. The furry, goofy-looking character is sometimes called "a seven-foot orange ball of beard." His chaotic antics are often displayed on the team's social media accounts. They include everything from swinging in from the ceiling before games to picking fights with other mascots.

GREATEST SEASONS

The 1973–74 Flyers averaged 22.2 penalty minutes per game. That was nearly eight more than any other team in the league. But behind the toughness was a high-scoring, talented squad that won 50 games.

Skilled shooter Rick MacLeish capped the year by clinching a Stanley Cup championship. He scored the only goal in a 1–0 game 6 victory over the Boston Bruins. Goaltender Bernie Parent did the rest by posting a shutout. Parent was at it again in game 6 of the 1974–75 Final against the Buffalo Sabres. The goaltender made 32 saves in a 2–0 win to clinch a second straight championship for Philadelphia.

Gritty quickly became one of the most popular mascots in the NHL.

PITTSBURGH PENGUINS

Despite stars like Jean Pronovost, the Pittsburgh Penguins had a losing record in each of their first seven seasons.

TEAM HISTORY

Since joining the NHL in 1967, the Pittsburgh Penguins have seen incredible highs but also terrifying lows. The team went bankrupt in 1975. But it later recovered and eventually claimed two Stanley Cup titles in the early 1990s, led by forwards Mario Lemieux and Jaromír Jágr.

In 1998, the Penguins went bankrupt again. This time, Lemieux stepped in and saved the team by buying it. In the mid-2000s, a new group of stars arrived. They were led by

A TALENTED HOUSE

Sidney Crosby entered the NHL in 2005 as the greatest young talent of his generation. But he needed a place to live. Mario Lemieux had the perfect solution. He invited the 18-year-old Crosby to live with him. Crosby stayed with the Lemieux family for five years as he developed into something that Lemieux had once been: the NHL's best player.

forwards Sidney Crosby and Evgeni Malkin, defenseman Kris Letang, and goaltender Marc-André Fleury. That core led the team to three more championships between 2009 and 2017.

GREATEST PLAYERS

- **Syl Apps Jr.**, C (1971–77)
- **Tom Barrasso**, G (1988–2000)
- **Sidney Crosby**, C (2005–)
- **Marc-André Fleury**, G (2003–17)
- **Ron Francis**, C (1991–98)
- **Jaromír Jágr**, RW (1990–2001)
- **Rick Kehoe**, RW (1974–84)
- **Mario Lemieux**, C (1984–97, 2000–06)
- **Kris Letang**, D (2006–)
- **Evgeni Malkin**, C (2006–)
- **Jean Pronovost**, RW (1968–78)
- **Kevin Stevens**, LW (1988–95, 2000–02)

Mario Lemieux gained the nickname "Super Mario" for his talent on the ice.

TEAM STATS AND RECORDS

ALL-TIME RECORD
- **Regular season:** 2027–1822–383–185
- **Postseason:** 212–186
- **Stanley Cup Final record:** 5–1

TOP COACHES
- **Dan Bylsma** (2009–14); 252–117–N/A–32 (regular season); 43–35 (postseason)
- **Mike Sullivan** (2015–); 375–219–N/A–77 (regular season); 44–38 (postseason)

CAREER OFFENSIVE LEADERS
- **Games played:** Sidney Crosby, 1,272
- **Goals:** Mario Lemieux, 690
- **Assists:** Mario Lemieux, 1,033
- **Points:** Mario Lemieux, 1,723
- **Penalty minutes:** Evgeni Malkin, 1,160
- **Hat tricks:** Mario Lemieux, 40
- **Shorthanded goals:** Mario Lemieux, 49
- **Power play goals:** Mario Lemieux, 236
- **Game-winning goals:** Sidney Crosby, 90

CAREER GOALTENDING LEADERS
- **Games played:** Marc-André Fleury, 691
- **Wins:** Marc-André Fleury, 375
- **Goals against average:** Marc-André Fleury, 2.58
- **Save percentage:** Matt Murray, .914
- **Shutouts:** Marc-André Fleury, 44

GREATEST SEASONS

In 1990–91, the Penguins won their first division title. Then, Mario Lemieux led the way on a thrilling playoff run. He tallied 44 points in 23 games. Lemieux capped it off by scoring a goal and adding three assists in an 8–0 rout of the Minnesota North Stars in game 6 of the Stanley Cup Final.

The 2008–09 Final pitted the upstart Penguins against the defending champion Detroit Red Wings. Pittsburgh held a 2–1 lead in the final seconds of game 7. Fleury's sprawling save of a shot by Detroit's Nicklas Lidström sealed the Penguins' third title. Crosby was just 21 that season, making him the youngest captain to ever hoist the Stanley Cup.

After several more years coming close, the Penguins made more Stanley Cup history in 2015–16 and 2016–17. The team won titles in both seasons. That made Pittsburgh the first back-to-back champions since the Red Wings in 1996–97 and 1997–98.

Sidney Crosby lifts the Stanley Cup after helping the Penguins win the championship in 2017. Crosby had one goal and six assists in the Final series.

SAN JOSE SHARKS

Right winger Owen Nolan was a star for the Sharks during the franchise's early years in the mid-1990s.

TEAM HISTORY

The NHL failed to catch on during its initial attempt to bring hockey to California's Bay Area in the 1970s. But the addition of the San Jose Sharks in 1991 turned out to be a smashing success. The team plays its home games at the always raucous SAP Center, which is commonly known as the "Shark Tank." The noisy arena was especially rocking during the 2000s and

2010s, when the Sharks were a yearly contender in the Western Conference. However, the team reached the Stanley Cup Final only once in that era.

The Sharks' period of success ended when veteran stars such as centers Joe Thornton and Patrick Marleau moved on in the late 2010s and early 2020s. The 2023–24 season marked San Jose's fifth straight out of the playoffs, and its 19 wins were the team's lowest since the franchise's early years.

GREATEST PLAYERS

- **Dan Boyle**, D (2008–14)
- **Brent Burns**, D (2011–22)
- **Logan Couture**, C (2009–)
- **Tomáš Hertl**, C (2013–24)
- **Erik Karlsson**, D (2018–23)
- **Patrick Marleau**, C (1997–2017, 2020–21)
- **Evgeni Nabokov**, G (2000–10)
- **Antti Niemi**, G (2010–15)
- **Owen Nolan**, RW (1995–2003)
- **Joe Pavelski**, C (2006–19)
- **Joe Thornton**, C (2005–20)
- **Marc-Édouard Vlasic**, D (2006–)

SHARKS IN THE WATER

San Jose really leans into the team's nickname at home games. When the players enter the ice for pregame warm-ups, they do so through the mouth of a huge shark head that is lowered to the ice. When San Jose goes on a power play, arena staffers play the theme song from the popular 1975 movie *Jaws*, which is about a killer shark, over the arena's loudspeakers.

TEAM STATS AND RECORDS

ALL-TIME RECORD
- **Regular season:** 1143–1055–121–201
- **Postseason:** 119–122
- **Stanley Cup Final record:** 0–1

TOP COACHES
- **Ron Wilson** (2002–08); 206–122–19–38 (regular season); 28–24 (postseason)
- **Todd McLellan** (2008–15); 311–163–N/A–66 (regular season, 30–32 (postseason)

CAREER OFFENSIVE LEADERS
- **Games played:** Patrick Marleau, 1,607
- **Goals:** Patrick Marleau, 522
- **Assists:** Joe Thornton, 804
- **Points:** Patrick Marleau, 1,111
- **Penalty minutes:** Jeff Odgers, 1,001
- **Hat tricks:** Jonathan Cheechoo, 9
- **Shorthanded goals:** Patrick Marleau, 17
- **Power play goals:** Patrick Marleau, 163
- **Game-winning goals:** Patrick Marleau, 101

CAREER GOALTENDING LEADERS
- **Games played:** Evgeni Nabokov, 563
- **Wins:** Evgeni Nabokov, 293
- **Goals against average:** Vesa Toskala, 2.35
- **Save percentage:** Antti Niemi, .917
- **Shutouts:** Evgeni Nabokov, 50

Center Joe Thornton knocks in the winning goal against the Los Angeles Kings in a 2011 playoff series.

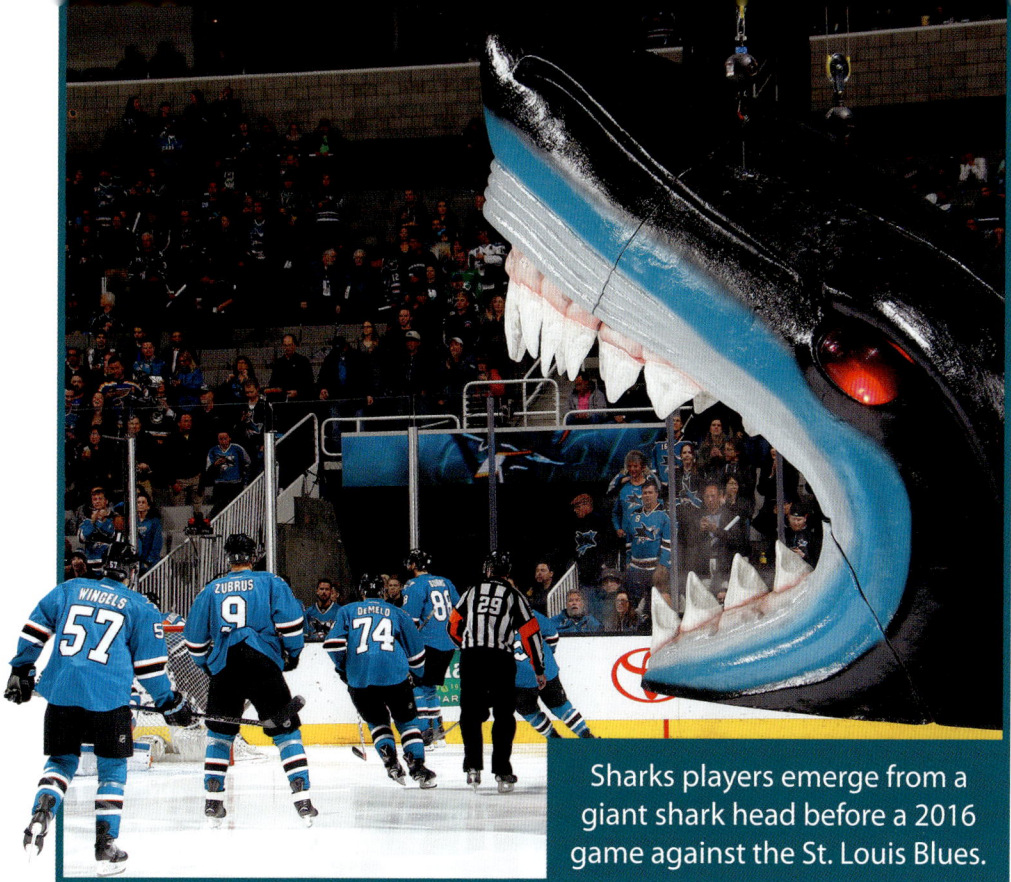

Sharks players emerge from a giant shark head before a 2016 game against the St. Louis Blues.

GREATEST SEASONS

A year after winning only 11 of 84 games in 1992–93, the Sharks were a surprise entrant into the 1993–94 NHL playoffs. They stunned the hockey world by upsetting the top-seeded Detroit Red Wings in a seven-game opening-round series. Center Jamie Baker's goal with 6:25 left in the game sealed a memorable 3–2 win in game 7.

In 2015–16, the Sharks were coming off a series of disappointing playoff exits. But led by new head coach Peter DeBoer, San Jose finally reached the Stanley Cup Final. Popular third-line winger Joel Ward scored twice in a 5–2 game 6 win over the St. Louis Blues to punch San Jose's ticket to the Final. There, the Sharks lost in six games to the Pittsburgh Penguins.

SEATTLE KRAKEN

Fans were invited to watch the Seattle Kraken Expansion Draft in 2021, where the team assembled its first roster.

TEAM HISTORY

When the NHL decided to add a thirty-second team before the 2021–22 season, Seattle was an easy choice. The city had a long history with professional and junior hockey. The Seattle Metropolitans played professional hockey in the PCHA in the 1910s and 1920s. In 1916–17, they became the first US team to win the Stanley Cup. The city even considered naming Seattle's new team the Metropolitans. But in the end, Kraken won out. The nickname comes from the mythical sea creature. The fictional Kraken resembles the real giant Pacific octopus that is found in the waters near Seattle.

GREATEST PLAYERS

- **Matthew Beniers**, C (2022–)
- **Oliver Bjorkstrand**, RW (2022–)
- **Vince Dunn**, D (2021–)
- **Jordan Eberle**, RW (2021–)
- **Yanni Gourde**, C (2021–)
- **Philipp Grubauer**, G (2021–)
- **Adam Larsson**, D (2021–)
- **Jared McCann**, C (2021–)
- **Jamie Oleksiak**, D (2021–)
- **Jaden Schwartz**, C (2021–)
- **Brandon Tanev**, LW (2021–)
- **Alexander Wennberg**, C (2021–24)

Canadian center Jared McCann came to the Kraken after playing with the Pittsburgh Penguins, and he soon became one of Seattle's top scorers.

TEAM STATS AND RECORDS

ALL-TIME RECORD
- **Regular season:** 107–112–0–27
- **Postseason:** 7–7
- **Stanley Cup Final record:** 0–0

TOP COACHES
- **Dave Hakstol** (2021–24); 107–112–N/A–27 (regular season); 7–7 (postseason)

CAREER OFFENSIVE LEADERS
- **Games played:** Adam Larsson, 245
- **Goals:** Jared McCann, 96
- **Assists:** Vince Dunn, 113
- **Points:** Jared McCann, 182
- **Penalty minutes:** Vince Dunn, 196
- **Hat tricks:** Jordan Eberle/Jared McCann, 1
- **Shorthanded goals:** Jared McCann, 6
- **Power play goals:** Jared McCann, 24
- **Game-winning goals:** Jordan Eberle/Alexander Wennberg, 9

CAREER GOALTENDING LEADERS
- **Games played:** Philipp Grubauer, 130
- **Wins:** Philipp Grubauer, 49
- **Goals against average:** Philipp Grubauer, 2.99
- **Save percentage:** Philipp Grubauer, .893
- **Shutouts:** Philipp Grubauer, 4

THE HORN FROM THE *HYAK*

Many ferry boats travel through the waters near Seattle. When the Kraken were looking for a goal horn, they borrowed one from a recently retired ferry boat. The MV *Hyak* carried passengers along the Washington coast from 1967 to 2019. Its horn is now blasted after every Kraken goal.

Defenseman Vince Dunn, *right*, moves in against Colorado Avalanche players in a 2023 first-round playoff game.

GREATEST SEASONS

The Kraken reached the playoffs in just their second season in 2022–23. But their reward was a first-round matchup with the defending champion Colorado Avalanche. Seattle's task got even harder when star forward Jared McCann was knocked out for the series by a hit from Colorado's Cale Makar in game 4. But Seattle rallied to eventually win in seven games.

    The Kraken nearly extended their run to the conference finals. They next faced the Dallas Stars. Seattle pushed the Stars to seven games in the second round before exiting the playoffs.

ST. LOUIS BLUES

Defenseman Bob Plager played for the Blues from the team's first season until 1978, reaching the playoffs almost every season in that span.

TEAM HISTORY

The St. Louis Blues found early success after they joined the NHL in 1967. The team played in the brand-new Western Division, which it won each of the team's first three years while competing against the other five expansion teams. The Blues' reward was to be thumped in the Stanley Cup Final without winning a single game in any of those seasons.

However, that successful start set the stage for St. Louis to become a yearly playoff contender. In fact, no team outside the Original Six has made the playoffs more than the Blues. But the ultimate prize of the Stanley Cup proved harder to come by. The Blues didn't return to the Stanley Cup Final until 2018–19. In that season, St. Louis finished the job to take home its only Stanley Cup title.

GREATEST PLAYERS

- **David Backes**, C (2006–16)
- **Bernie Federko**, C (1976–89)
- **Brett Hull**, RW (1988–98)
- **Al MacInnis**, D (1994–2003)
- **Alex Pietrangelo**, D (2008–20)
- **Bob Plager**, D (1967–78)
- **Chris Pronger**, D (1995–2004)
- **Alexander Steen**, C (2008–20)
- **Brian Sutter**, LW (1976–88)
- **Vladimir Tarasenko**, RW (2012–23)
- **Keith Tkachuk**, LW (2001–10)
- **Garry Unger**, C (1971–79)

Left winger Keith Tkachuk had almost ten years of NHL experience before joining the Blues, and he soon became a difference maker for the team.

TEAM STATS AND RECORDS

ALL-TIME RECORD

- **Regular season:** 2058–1738–432–191
- **Postseason:** 188–228
- **Stanley Cup Final record:** 1–3

TOP COACHES

- **Joel Quenneville** (1996–2004); 307–191–77–18 (regular season); 34–34 (postseason)
- **Craig Berube** (2018–23); 206–132–N/A–44 (regular season); 24–27 (postseason)

CAREER OFFENSIVE LEADERS

- **Games played:** Bernie Federko, 927
- **Goals:** Brett Hull, 527
- **Assists:** Bernie Federko, 721
- **Points:** Bernie Federko, 1,073
- **Penalty minutes:** Brian Sutter, 1,786
- **Hat tricks:** Brett Hull, 27
- **Shorthanded goals:** Larry Patey, 23
- **Power play goals:** Brett Hull, 195
- **Game-winning goals:** Brett Hull, 70

CAREER GOALTENDING LEADERS

- **Games played:** Mike Liut, 347
- **Wins:** Mike Liut, 151
- **Goals against average:** Brian Elliott, 2.01
- **Save percentage:** Brian Elliott, .925
- **Shutouts:** Brian Elliott, 25

GREATEST SEASONS

On January 3, 2019, the Blues were in last place in the Western Conference. The playoffs looked like a faraway dream. But the team finished the season on a 26–9–4 run backstopped by new goaltender Jordan Binnington.

Jordan Binnington's spectacular goaltending helped propel the Blues to a Stanley Cup championship in 2019.

Binnington had been called up midseason from the minor leagues. He continued to shine as the Blues survived four tough postseason series. On June 12, goals from Ryan O'Reilly, Alex Pietrangelo, Brayden Schenn, and Zach Sanford polished off the Boston Bruins in a 4–1 game 7 victory. St. Louis finally had a Stanley Cup championship.

LAILA

Laila Anderson was 11 years old during the Blues' Stanley Cup run in 2019. A huge fan of the team, Laila was also suffering from a life-threatening autoimmune disease. The Blues kept Laila involved with the team throughout the run. She was even on the ice to celebrate the game 7 victory. Laila survived, and she even won a Missouri state championship as a 15-year-old hockey player in 2024.

TAMPA BAY LIGHTNING

Steven Stamkos, *center*, and Martin St. Louis, *left*, celebrate a goal in a 2012 game against the Washington Capitals.

TEAM HISTORY

The Tampa Bay Lightning joined the NHL in 1992–93. The team's first decade wasn't pretty. The Lightning reached the playoffs only once in that span. In four of those years, they won fewer than 20 games. But fiery head coach John Tortorella's arrival late in the 2000–01 season sparked a turnaround.

Three years later, the Lightning won their first Stanley Cup after beating the Calgary Flames in seven games. Another downturn was right around the corner, but Tampa Bay reemerged in the late 2010s as one of the NHL's most exciting teams. A high-flying offensive group added back-to-back titles in 2019–20 and 2020–21.

GREATEST PLAYERS

- **Dan Boyle**, D (2002–08)
- **Victor Hedman**, D (2009–)
- **Nikolai Khabibulin**, G (2000–04)
- **Alex Killorn**, C/LW (2013–23)
- **Nikita Kucherov**, RW (2013–)
- **Vincent Lecavalier**, C (1998–2013)
- **Ondřej Palát**, LW (2013–22)
- **Brayden Point**, C (2016–)
- **Brad Richards**, C (2000–08)
- **Martin St. Louis**, RW (2000–14)
- **Steven Stamkos**, C (2008–24)
- **Andrei Vasilevskiy**, G (2014–)

MANON RHÉAUME

Manon Rhéaume was a star goalie for Canada's women's national team during the 1990s. In 1992, Rhéaume suited up for the Lightning in a preseason game against the St. Louis Blues and stopped seven of nine shots in one period. She appeared in a Tampa Bay preseason game again a year later against the Boston Bruins. Rhéaume was the first woman to play for an NHL team.

TEAM STATS AND RECORDS

ALL-TIME RECORD
- **Regular season:** 1127–1029–112–172
- **Postseason:** 124–95
- **Stanley Cup Final record:** 3–2

TOP COACHES
- **John Tortorella** (2001–08); 239–222–36–38 (regular season); 24–21 (postseason)
- **John Cooper** (2013–); 525–279–N/A–75 (regular season); 87–63 (postseason)

CAREER OFFENSIVE LEADERS
- **Games played:** Steven Stamkos, 1,082
- **Goals:** Steven Stamkos, 555
- **Assists:** Martin St. Louis, 588
- **Points:** Steven Stamkos, 1,137
- **Penalty minutes:** Chris Gratton, 828
- **Hat tricks:** Steven Stamkos, 13
- **Shorthanded goals:** Martin St. Louis, 28
- **Power play goals:** Steven Stamkos, 214
- **Game-winning goals:** Steven Stamkos, 85

CAREER GOALTENDING LEADERS
- **Games played:** Andrei Vasilevskiy, 477
- **Wins:** Andrei Vasilevskiy, 293
- **Goals against average:** Ben Bishop, 2.28
- **Save percentage:** Ben Bishop, .921
- **Shutouts:** Andrei Vasilevskiy, 34

GREATEST SEASONS

The Lightning hoisted their second Stanley Cup in 2019–20. Unfortunately their fans couldn't be there to celebrate with the team. Due to the COVID-19 pandemic, all NHL playoff games

Goaltender Andrei Vasilevskiy was a part of the Lightning's back-to-back Stanley Cup victories in 2020 and 2021.

that year had been moved to either Toronto or Edmonton, and no fans were allowed in the arenas.

The next year, the Lightning were back home and back in the playoffs. The star of the show was goaltender Andrei Vasilevskiy. The eventual Conn Smythe Trophy winner shut out the New York Islanders 1–0 in game 7 to push Tampa Bay to the Stanley Cup Final. In game 5, he backstopped the Lightning to another 1–0 win over the Montreal Canadiens to clinch the Cup. Tampa Bay became just the second team to repeat as champions in the 2000s.

Right winger Nikita Kucherov led the NHL in scoring in 2023–24 with a Tampa Bay–record 144 points.

TORONTO MAPLE LEAFS

Toronto's Syl Apps, *center*, celebrates with head coach Hap Day, *left*, and team manager Conn Smythe, *right*, after winning the Stanley Cup in 1948.

TEAM HISTORY

Only the Montreal Canadiens have won more Stanley Cups than the Toronto Maple Leafs' 13 titles. But Toronto's history is much more complicated. Though the team shone during the Original Six era, Toronto's last title came in 1966–67, the season before the league expanded to 12 teams.

Since then, the Maple Leafs' quest for another title has become a yearly story in the NHL. The fact that the team plays in Canada's biggest city doesn't help. The hockey-obsessed fans of Toronto put a lot of pressure on the Leafs. Star players such as Darryl Sittler, Mats Sundin, and Auston Matthews have provided plenty of star power over the years. But what die-hard Toronto fans really want is another Stanley Cup.

GREATEST PLAYERS

- **Syl Apps**, C (1936–48)
- **Johnny Bower**, G (1958–69)
- **Turk Broda**, G (1936–52)
- **Charlie Conacher**, RW (1929–38)
- **Tim Horton**, D (1950–70)
- **Dave Keon**, C (1960–75)
- **Frank Mahovlich**, LW (1957–68)
- **Mitch Marner**, RW (2016–)
- **Auston Matthews**, C (2016–)
- **Börje Salming**, D (1973–89)
- **Darryl Sittler**, C (1970–82)
- **Mats Sundin**, C (1995–2008)

Defenseman Tim Horton skates between two Montreal Canadiens in a 1967 game.

TEAM STATS AND RECORDS

ALL-TIME RECORD
- **Regular season:** 3150–2897–783–202
- **Postseason:** 272–302
- **Stanley Cup Final record:** 13–8

TOP COACHES
- **Hap Day** (1940–50); 259–206–81–N/A (regular season); 49–31 (postseason)
- **Punch Imlach** (1958–69, 1980); 370–275–125–N/A (regular season); 44–48 (postseason)

CAREER OFFENSIVE LEADERS
- **Games played:** George Armstrong, 1,188
- **Goals:** Mats Sundin, 420
- **Assists:** Börje Salming, 620
- **Points:** Mats Sundin, 987
- **Penalty minutes:** Tie Domi, 2,265
- **Hat tricks:** Darryl Sittler, 18
- **Shorthanded goals:** Dave Keon, 31
- **Power play goals:** Mats Sundin, 124
- **Game-winning goals:** Mats Sundin, 79

CAREER GOALTENDING LEADERS
- **Games played:** Turk Broda, 629
- **Wins:** Turk Broda, 304
- **Goals against average:** Al Rollins, 2.04
- **Save percentage:** Jacques Plante, .925
- **Shutouts:** Turk Broda, 61

AN EVOLVING NAME

Toronto's original nickname was the Arenas, but the nickname was never official. In 1919, the team was renamed the St. Patricks. That nickname lasted for eight years. Then Conn Smythe bought the St. Patricks and renamed them the Maple Leafs. He got the nickname from Canada's World War I soldiers, who wore the symbol on their uniforms.

GREATEST SEASONS

The 1941–42 Stanley Cup Final started poorly for the Maple Leafs. Toronto lost the first three games to the Detroit Red Wings. But in game 4 Nick Metz scored late in a 4–3 victory to keep Toronto alive. Then, star forward Syl Apps and Nick's brother Don Metz each had five points in a 9–3 blowout in game 5. Goaltender Turk Broda's 3–0 shutout in game 6 evened the series.

After Detroit took a 1–0 lead in game 7, Toronto rallied again. Pete Langelle's goal near the midway point of the third period proved to be the game winner in an eventual 3–1 Toronto victory. Nearly 80 years later, the Maple Leafs were still the only team to ever come from 3–0 down to win a Stanley Cup Final.

> Center Mats Sundin got his start in the NHL with the Quebec Nordiques, but he played most of his legendary career with the Maple Leafs.

UTAH HOCKEY CLUB

TEAM HISTORY

The Utah Hockey Club was founded in 1971 as the Winnipeg Jets. The team played in the WHA before joining the NHL in 1979. Through the 1980s and the early 1990s the Jets played in front of passionate fans. But the team struggled financially and moved south to Phoenix, Arizona, after the 1995–96 season to become the Coyotes.

Despite a few successful seasons, the Coyotes often struggled off the ice during their time in the desert. The franchise went bankrupt in 2009, and the league took over control of the team. After years of relocation rumors, the franchise moved north to Salt Lake City, Utah, in the summer of 2024. The team used the name Utah Hockey Club for its first season. It planned to establish a permanent identity the following year.

Center Thomas Steen helped the Winnipeg Jets reach the playoffs 10 times in his 14 seasons with the franchise in the 1980s and 1990s.

GREATEST PLAYERS

- **Shane Doan**, RW (1995–2017)
- **Oliver Ekman-Larsson**, D (2010–21)
- **Dale Hawerchuk**, C (1981–90)
- **Clayton Keller**, C (2017–)
- **Nikolai Khabibulin**, G (1995–99)
- **Paul MacLean**, RW (1981–88)
- **Teppo Numminen**, D (1988–2003)
- **Jeremy Roenick**, C (1996–2001, 2006–07)
- **Doug Smail**, LW (1980–91)
- **Mike Smith**, G (2011–17)
- **Thomas Steen**, C (1981–95)
- **Keith Tkachuk**, LW (1992–2001)

Goaltender Mike Smith had a .944 save percentage during the Coyotes' playoff run in 2011–12.

TEAM STATS AND RECORDS
ALL-TIME RECORD
- **Regular season:** 1424–1599–266–191
- **Postseason:** 45–83
- **Stanley Cup Final record:** 0–0

TOP COACHES
- **Bobby Francis** (2000–04); 165–144–60–21 (regular season); 2–8 (postseason)
- **Dave Tippett** (2010–17); 282–257–N/A–83 (regular season); 12–15 (postseason)

CAREER OFFENSIVE LEADERS
- **Games played:** Shane Doan, 1,540
- **Goals:** Shane Doan, 402
- **Assists:** Shane Doan, 570
- **Points:** Shane Doan, 972
- **Penalty minutes:** Keith Tkachuk, 1,508
- **Hat tricks:** Dale Hawerchuk, 12
- **Shorthanded goals:** Doug Smail, 25
- **Power play goals:** Shane Doan, 128
- **Game-winning goals:** Shane Doan, 69

CAREER GOALTENDING LEADERS
- **Games played:** Mike Smith, 312
- **Wins:** Ilya Bryzgalov, 130
- **Goals against average:** Sean Burke, 2.39
- **Save percentage:** Antti Raanta, .921
- **Shutouts:** Mike Smith, 22

GREATEST SEASONS
Over 27 seasons in Arizona, the Coyotes made the playoffs just nine times. Their most memorable run came in 2011–12. The team won its first-ever division title. Arizona then surprised the Chicago Blackhawks with a win in the opening round of the playoffs. It was the franchise's first series win since 1987.

The Delta Center in Salt Lake City, Utah, held a ceremony to welcome the city's new NHL team in April 2024.

Arizona's season finally ended with a loss to the eventual Stanley Cup champions, the Los Angeles Kings, in the Western Conference finals.

THE WHITEOUT

In 1987, the Winnipeg Jets encouraged their fans to wear all white to a playoff game against the Calgary Flames. It soon became a team tradition in the playoffs. When the team moved to Arizona, Coyotes fans continued the whiteout tradition. The new version of the Winnipeg Jets, which began play in 2011, also does this. Other NHL teams have copied the idea as well.

VANCOUVER CANUCKS

TEAM HISTORY

Vancouver was frustrated to not receive one of the six new NHL expansion teams in 1967. The city had a proud hockey history dating back to the Vancouver Millionaires of the PCHA. This team won the Stanley Cup in 1914–15. Still, the NHL came to the city not long after the 1967 expansion. The Canucks formed in time for the 1970–71 season. Like their expansion partners the Buffalo Sabres, the Canucks were still looking for their first Stanley Cup more than 50 years later. The two franchises share the record for the longest time in the league without a championship. For their part, the Canucks have reached the Final three times. In two of them, they lost in seven games.

After his playing career, Thomas Gradin joined the Canucks staff as a scout, helping to find talented new players.

Identical twin brothers Henrik, *left*, and Daniel Sedin both played 17 seasons for the Canucks.

GREATEST PLAYERS

- **Kevin Bieksa**, D (2005–15)
- **Pavel Bure**, RW (1991–98)
- **Alexander Edler**, D (2006–21)
- **Thomas Gradin**, C (1978–86)
- **Trevor Linden**, RW (1988–97, 2001–08)
- **Roberto Luongo**, G (2006–14)
- **Kirk McLean**, G (1987–98)
- **Markus Näslund**, LW (1996–2008)
- **Daniel Sedin**, LW (2000–18)
- **Henrik Sedin**, C (2000–18)
- **Stan Smyl**, RW (1978–91)
- **Tony Tanti**, RW (1982–90)

TEAM STATS AND RECORDS

ALL-TIME RECORD

- **Regular season:** 1777–1836–391–187
- **Postseason:** 118–141
- **Stanley Cup Final record:** 0–3

TOP COACHES

- **Pat Quinn** (1991–96); 141–111–28–N/A (regular season); 31–30 (postseason)
- **Alain Vigneault** (2006–13); 313–170–N/A–57 (regular season); 33–35 (postseason)

CAREER OFFENSIVE LEADERS

- **Games played:** Henrik Sedin, 1,330
- **Goals:** Daniel Sedin, 393
- **Assists:** Henrik Sedin, 830
- **Points:** Henrik Sedin, 1,070
- **Penalty minutes:** Gino Odjick, 2,127
- **Hat tricks:** Markus Näslund/Tony Tanti, 10
- **Shorthanded goals:** Pavel Bure, 24
- **Power play goals:** Daniel Sedin, 138
- **Game-winning goals:** Daniel Sedin, 86

CAREER GOALTENDING LEADERS

- **Games played:** Kirk McLean, 516
- **Wins:** Roberto Luongo, 252
- **Goals against average:** Cory Schneider, 2.20
- **Save percentage:** Cory Schneider, .927
- **Shutouts:** Roberto Luongo, 38

GREATEST SEASONS

The Canucks reached the Stanley Cup Final in 1981–82 and 1993–94. But both of those runs came as determined underdogs. The 2010–11 Canucks finished the season with a league-best total of 54 wins. Forward Alexandre Burrows then

Defenseman Alexander Edler races away from a Boston Bruins player during the 2011 Stanley Cup Final.

scored a dramatic overtime winner in game 7 of the opening round of the playoffs. The goal knocked out the defending champion Chicago Blackhawks.

Vancouver eventually reached the Final against the Boston Bruins. In a rugged seven-game series, Boston came out on top. The mood soon turned sour in Vancouver. A riot in the city after the game caused $4 million in damage.

WHY NOT BOTH?

In 1999, a pair of teenage Swedish stars were ready to be drafted into the NHL. They also happened to be twin brothers. Vancouver owned the third pick in the draft, and general manager Brian Burke swung a trade with the Atlanta Thrashers to get the second pick too. The team took Daniel Sedin second and brother Henrik third. The two superstars went on to become the two top scorers in Canucks history.

VEGAS GOLDEN KNIGHTS

TEAM HISTORY

The Vegas Golden Knights made a huge splash when they joined the NHL in 2017–18. While most expansion teams struggle, the Golden Knights were a powerhouse right away. The team won 51 games and reached the Stanley Cup Final in its first season.

Though the team didn't win, Vegas quickly became a destination for top players. Aggressive general managers George McPhee and later Kelly McCrimmon made several moves to bring in top stars like Mark Stone, Max Pacioretty, and Jack Eichel. Those risks paid off, as the Golden Knights went back to the Stanley Cup Final in 2022–23. This time, Vegas skated away with the Cup.

Center William Karlsson was one of many players the Golden Knights picked in the 2017 NHL Expansion Draft who became key pieces of Vegas's surprising first season.

GREATEST PLAYERS

- **Jack Eichel**, C (2021–)
- **Marc-André Fleury**, G (2017–21)
- **William Karlsson**, C (2017–)
- **Jonathan Marchessault**, C (2017–24)
- **Brayden McNabb**, D (2017–)
- **Max Pacioretty**, LW (2018–22)
- **Alex Pietrangelo**, D (2020–)
- **Reilly Smith**, RW (2017–23)
- **Chandler Stephenson**, C (2019–24)
- **Mark Stone**, RW (2019–)
- **Shea Theodore**, D (2017–)
- **Alex Tuch**, RW (2017–21)

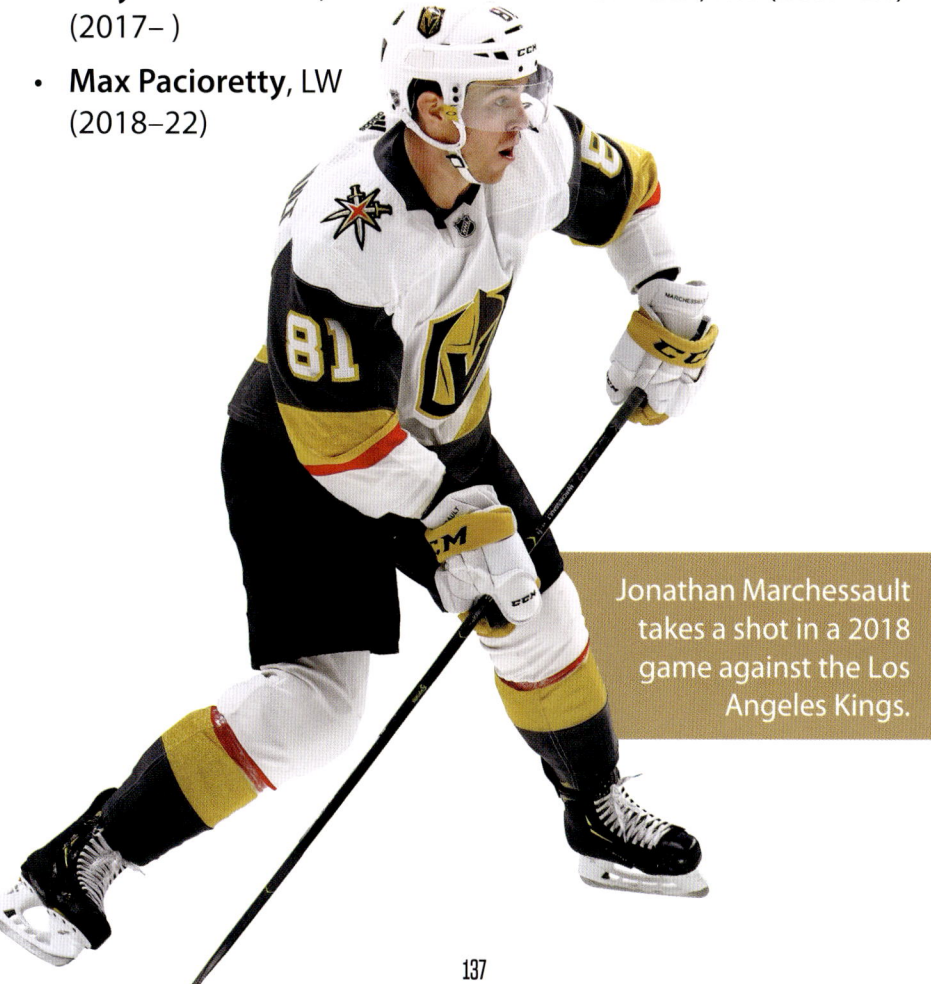

Jonathan Marchessault takes a shot in a 2018 game against the Los Angeles Kings.

TEAM STATS AND RECORDS

ALL-TIME RECORD
- **Regular season**: 312–176–0–49
- **Postseason**: 57–38
- **Stanley Cup Final record**: 1–1

TOP COACHES
- **Gerrard Gallant** (2017–20); 213–118–N/A–75 (regular season); 16–11 (postseason)
- **Bruce Cassidy** (2022–); 96–51–N/A–17 (regular season); 19–10 (postseason)

CAREER OFFENSIVE LEADERS
- **Games played**: Jonathan Marchessault, 514
- **Goals**: Jonathan Marchessault, 192
- **Assists**: Jonathan Marchessault, 225
- **Points**: Jonathan Marchessault, 417
- **Penalty minutes**: Brayden McNabb, 290
- **Hat tricks**: Jonathan Marchessault, 5
- **Shorthanded goals**: William Karlsson/Reilly Smith, 12
- **Power play goals**: Jonathan Marchessault, 42
- **Game-winning goals**: Jonathan Marchessault, 32

CAREER GOALTENDING LEADERS
- **Games played**: Marc-André Fleury, 192
- **Wins**: Marc-André Fleury, 117
- **Goals against average**: Marc-André Fleury, 2.41
- **Save percentage**: Marc-André Fleury, .917
- **Shutouts**: Marc-André Fleury, 23

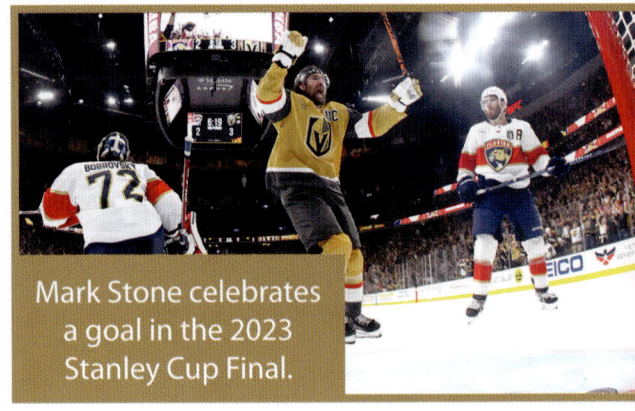

Mark Stone celebrates a goal in the 2023 Stanley Cup Final.

A REAL VEGAS SHOW

Before Vegas's first game of the 2017–18 Stanley Cup playoffs, fans were treated to a show. A man dressed as a Golden Knight skated to center ice. Soon, he engaged in a choreographed battle with a mascot representing the Los Angeles Kings, their first-round opponent. The show was a hit.

GREATEST SEASONS

Few expected the Golden Knights to reach the Stanley Cup Final in their first season. But they did, dominating the Western Conference. Vegas lost only three games in three playoff rounds to reach the Final against the Washington Capitals.

Five years later, the Knights went on a similar run. This time coach Bruce Cassidy's team lost only five games in three rounds while knocking out the Winnipeg Jets, Edmonton Oilers, and Dallas Stars. In the Final, Mark Stone had nine points in five games. This helped finish off the Golden Knights' 4–1 victory over the Florida Panthers.

The Golden Knights have become famous for their elaborate pregame shows.

WASHINGTON CAPITALS

TEAM HISTORY

The Washington Capitals team that joined the NHL in 1974–75 was one of the worst the league had ever seen. The team won only eight of 80 games all year. It took a while for things to get better.

The US capital city didn't have a winning team until 1982–83. However, struggling in the 2003–04 season actually helped Washington. That allowed the Capitals to select future superstar Alex Ovechkin with the top pick in that year's draft. One of the league's all-time great goal scorers, he turned Washington into a true contender. After years of playoff disappointment, it all came together in 2017–18. That year, the Capitals beat the upstart Vegas Golden Knights to win their first Stanley Cup title.

Defenseman Rod Langway's tough play earned him the nickname "The Secretary of Defense."

GREATEST PLAYERS

- **Nicklas Bäckström**, C (2007–)
- **Peter Bondra**, RW (1990–2004)
- **John Carlson**, D (2009–)
- **Mike Gartner**, RW (1979–89)
- **Sergei Gonchar**, D (1995–2004)
- **Braden Holtby**, G (2010–20)
- **Dale Hunter**, C (1987–99)
- **Calle Johansson**, D (1989–2003)
- **Olaf Kölzig**, D (1989, 1993–2008)
- **Rod Langway**, D (1982–93)
- **Alex Ovechkin**, LW (2005–)
- **Michal Pivoňka**, C (1986–99)

Alex Ovechkin launches a shot in a 2009 game against the Philadelphia Flyers.

TEAM STATS AND RECORDS

ALL-TIME RECORD
- **Regular season:** 1819–1561–303–196
- **Postseason:** 140–165
- **Stanley Cup Final record:** 1–1

TOP COACHES
- **Bryan Murray** (1981–90); 343–246–83–N/A (regular season); 24–29 (postseason)
- **Barry Trotz** (2014–18); 205–89–N/A–34 (regular season); 36–27 (postseason)

CAREER OFFENSIVE LEADERS
- **Games played:** Alex Ovechkin, 1,426
- **Goals:** Alex Ovechkin, 853
- **Assists:** Nicklas Bäckström, 762
- **Points:** Alex Ovechkin, 1,550
- **Penalty minutes:** Dale Hunter, 2,003
- **Hat tricks:** Alex Ovechkin, 30
- **Shorthanded goals:** Peter Bondra, 32
- **Power play goals:** Alex Ovechkin, 312
- **Game-winning goals:** Alex Ovechkin, 129

CAREER GOALTENDING LEADERS
- **Games played:** Olaf Kölzig, 711
- **Wins:** Olaf Kölzig, 301
- **Goals against average:** Philipp Grubauer, 2.29
- **Save percentage:** Philipp Grubauer, .923
- **Shutouts:** Braden Holtby/Olaf Kölzig, 35

GREATEST SEASONS

Though Alex Ovechkin won the Conn Smythe Trophy after Washington's Cup run in 2018, goaltender Braden Holtby played a huge role as well. The 28-year-old goaltender put up shutouts in both game 6 and game 7 of the Eastern Conference

Goaltender Braden Holtby's game 2 heroics helped the Capitals overcome the Golden Knights in the 2018 Stanley Cup Final.

finals to knock out the Tampa Bay Lightning. With two minutes to go in game 2 of the Final, Washington held a 3–2 lead over the Vegas Golden Knights. Holtby made a sprawling stick save on Vegas forward Alex Tuch to keep it that way. "The Save" helped Washington even the series at 1–1. The Capitals then won the next three games to claim the title.

TROPHY HAUL

Capitals star Alex Ovechkin had a great season in 2007–08. His league-leading 65 goals earned him the Rocket Richard Trophy as the league's top scorer. And he took home the Art Ross Trophy for leading the NHL with 112 points. Ovechkin also won the Lester B. Pearson Award (now known as the Ted Lindsay Award) and the Hart Memorial Trophy. That made him the only player in NHL history to win all four honors in the same season.

WINNIPEG JETS

TEAM HISTORY

Most of the time when NHL teams have moved in the 2000s, it has been from a northern city to a southern city. That trend was reversed in 2011 when the Atlanta Thrashers moved north to Winnipeg. In 11 seasons in Georgia, the team had never won a playoff game. And with attendance lagging, the team needed a new home.

The city welcomed Atlanta's franchise before the 2011–12 season. Winnipeg had lost the original Jets to Phoenix in 1996. Since the Phoenix Coyotes didn't keep the rights to the Jets nickname, Winnipeg was able to use it again. That was music to the ears of the team's passionate fans. Though Winnipeg is one of the league's smallest cities, the Jets played in front of full-house crowds for eight consecutive years after hockey returned.

One of the team's biggest stars during its Atlanta years was high-scoring left winger Ilya Kovalchuk.

GREATEST PLAYERS

- **Dustin Byfuglien**, D (2010–19)
- **Kyle Connor**, LW (2016–)
- **Nikolaj Ehlers**, LW (2015–)
- **Toby Enström**, D (2007–18)
- **Connor Hellebuyck**, G (2015–)
- **Ilya Kovalchuk**, LW (2001–10)
- **Vyacheslav Kozlov**, LW (2002–10)
- **Bryan Little**, RW (2007–19)
- **Josh Morrissey**, D (2016–)
- **Ondřej Pavelec**, G (2007–17)
- **Mark Scheifele**, C (2011, 2013–)
- **Blake Wheeler**, RW (2011–23)

Goaltender Connor Hellebuyck was a surprise success after joining the Jets in 2015.

WINNIPEG JETS

HOT TICKET

Even though the original Jets left in the 1990s, it was not because Winnipeg fans weren't passionate about the team. They proved that again when season tickets went on sale once the Thrashers moved to Winnipeg. Season ticket packages for the new Jets sold out in just 17 minutes.

TEAM STATS AND RECORDS

ALL-TIME RECORD
- **Regular season:** 861–818–45–173
- **Postseason:** 18–35
- **Stanley Cup Final record:** 0–0

TOP COACHES
- **Paul Maurice** (2014–22); 315–223–N/A–62 (regular season); 16–23 (postseason)
- **Rick Bowness** (2022–24); 98–57–N/A–9 (regular season); 2–8 (postseason)

CAREER OFFENSIVE LEADERS
- **Games played:** Blake Wheeler, 897
- **Goals:** Ilya Kovalchuk, 328
- **Assists:** Blake Wheeler, 550
- **Points:** Blake Wheeler, 812
- **Penalty minutes:** Chris Thorburn, 832
- **Hat tricks:** Ilya Kovalchuk, 11
- **Shorthanded goals:** Marián Hossa, 12
- **Power play goals:** Ilya Kovalchuk, 115
- **Game-winning goals:** Kyle Connor, 52

CAREER GOALTENDING LEADERS
- **Games played:** Connor Hellebuyck, 505
- **Wins:** Connor Hellebuyck, 275
- **Goals against average:** Laurent Brossoit, 2.51
- **Save percentage:** Laurent Brossoit/Connor Hellebuyck, .917
- **Shutouts:** Connor Hellebuyck, 37

Center Paul Stastny maneuvers with the puck against the Golden Knights during their 2018 playoff series.

GREATEST SEASONS

Going into 2017–18, the Jets had made only one playoff appearance in six seasons. But the team was seeing big improvements. It reached 50 wins for the first time since the Atlanta Thrashers were founded in 1999.

After knocking off the Minnesota Wild in the opening round, Winnipeg survived a tense seven-game series against the Nashville Predators. The Jets took game 7 by a 5–1 score behind two goals and an assist from center Paul Stastny. Winnipeg won game 1 of the Western Conference finals at home against the Vegas Golden Knights. However, four straight losses finished off the Jets' best season yet.

STAR PLAYERS

JEAN BÉLIVEAU C
Montreal Canadiens (1950–51, 1952–71)

Known as *Le Gros Bill*, meaning "Big Bill," Jean Béliveau was hailed for his skills, strength, and graceful leadership. Béliveau was a member of ten Stanley Cup champions as a Montreal Canadiens player. He then became a team executive for seven more Cups. No person's name appears on the famous trophy more than Béliveau's.

Jean Béliveau

Games: 1,125 **Points:** 1,219
Goals: 507 **Stanley**
Assists: 712 **Cups:** 10
Awards: One Art Ross Trophy, two Hart Trophies, one Conn Smythe Trophy

MIKE BOSSY RW
New York Islanders (1977–87)

Mike Bossy was the first rookie to score 50 goals in a season. He went on to score at least 50 goals in each of his next eight seasons too. The speedy skater's streak of nine straight 50-goal seasons is still a record. Sadly, a back injury that caused persistent pain forced him to retire at age 30.

Games: 752 **Points:** 1,126
Goals: 573 **Stanley**
Assists: 553 **Cups:** 4
Awards: One Calder Trophy, one Conn Smythe Trophy, three Lady Byng Trophies

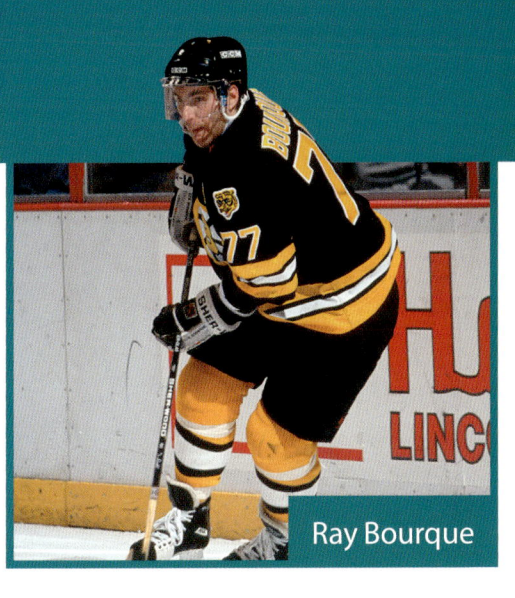
Ray Bourque

RAY BOURQUE D
Boston Bruins (1979–2000), Colorado Avalanche (2000–01)

A steady, adaptable defenseman, Ray Bourque was the backbone of the Boston Bruins for two decades. But his teams routinely came up short of the Stanley Cup. With his career nearing an end, Bourque was traded to the contending Colorado Avalanche in 2000. Most of the hockey world cheered him on as he won the 2001 Stanley Cup championship in his final season.

Games: 1,612
Goals: 410
Assists: 1,169
Points: 1,579
Stanley Cups: 1
Awards: One Calder Trophy, five Norris Trophies

Mike Bossy

STAR PLAYERS

Johnny Bower

Games: 552
Wins-Losses-Ties: 250–192–90
Goals against average: 2.51
Save percentage: .922
Shutouts: 37
Stanley Cups: 4
Awards: Two Vezina Trophies

JOHNNY BOWER G
New York Rangers (1953–56), Toronto Maple Leafs (1958–69)

Johnny Bower didn't start playing in the NHL until he was 29 years old. He played well into his forties, long enough to backstop the Toronto Maple Leafs to four Stanley Cups in the 1960s. Legendary center Jean Béliveau said Bower was the toughest goalie to deke in the league.

MARTIN BRODEUR G
New Jersey Devils (1991–92, 1993–2014), St. Louis Blues (2014–15)

Martin Brodeur retired as the all-time winningest goaltender in NHL history. His shot stopping was elite. But Brodeur was also such

Martin Brodeur

Games: 1,266
Wins-Losses-Ties/ Overtime Losses: 691–397–154
Goals against average: 2.24
Save percentage: .912
Shutouts: 125
Stanley Cups: 3
Awards: One Calder Trophy, four Vezina Trophies

a good puck handler and passer that the league changed its rules to prevent goaltenders from playing the puck in certain areas of the ice.

CHRIS CHELIOS D
Montreal Canadiens (1984–90), Chicago Blackhawks (1990–99), Detroit Red Wings (1999–2009), Atlanta Thrashers (2010)

Defenseman Chris Chelios played an impressive 26 seasons in the NHL. In only two of them did his teams miss the playoffs. The tough, steady Chelios's 266 postseason games were an NHL record when he finally retired at age 48.

Games: 1,651
Goals: 185
Assists: 763
Points: 948
Stanley Cups: 3
Awards: Three Norris Trophies

Chris Chelios

PAUL COFFEY D

Edmonton Oilers (1980–87), Pittsburgh Penguins (1987–92), Los Angeles Kings (1992–93), Detroit Red Wings (1993–96), Hartford Whalers/Carolina Hurricanes (1996, 1998–2000), Philadelphia Flyers (1996–98), Chicago Blackhawks (1998), Boston Bruins (2000)

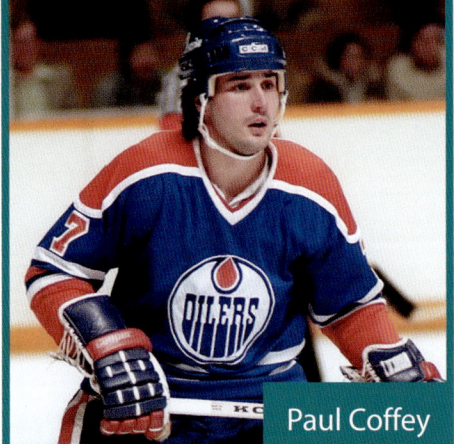
Paul Coffey

Games: 1,409　**Points:** 1,531
Goals: 396　**Stanley Cups:** 4
Assists: 1,135
Awards: Three Norris Trophies

Paul Coffey was a defenseman who played like a forward. He used his speed to fly up the ice, and his booming shots helped him score like no defenseman had before. Coffey's 48 goals in 1985–86 set a new record for blueliners.

SIDNEY CROSBY C

Pittsburgh Penguins (2005–)

Sidney Crosby entered the NHL in 2005 as the most hyped player since Wayne Gretzky. He certainly lived up to the billing. He became the youngest player to top 100 points in a season in his rookie year. In 2009, the 21-year-old became the youngest team captain to hoist the Stanley Cup.

Games: 1,272　**Assists:** 1,004　**Stanley Cups:** 3
Goals: 592　**Points:** 1,596
Awards: Two Art Ross Trophies, two Conn Smythe Trophies, two Hart Memorial Trophies

Pavel Datsyuk

Sidney Crosby

PAVEL DATSYUK C
Detroit Red Wings (2001–16)

Pavel Datsyuk, the Russian "Magic Man," could make opposing defenders and goaltenders look silly with his incredible stickhandling ability. The underrated Datsyuk won seven major awards and two Stanley Cups.

Games: 953 **Points:** 918
Goals: 314 **Stanley Cups:** 2
Assists: 604
Awards: Three Selke Trophies, four Lady Byng Trophies

STAR PLAYERS

Marcel Dionne

Games: 1,348 **Points:** 1,771
Goals: 731 **Stanley**
Assists: 1,040 **Cups:** 0
Awards: One Art Ross Trophy, two Lady Byng Trophies

MARCEL DIONNE C
Detroit Red Wings (1971–75), Los Angeles Kings (1975–87), New York Rangers (1987–89)

Pat Quinn, one of Marcel Dionne's coaches with the Los Angeles Kings, dubbed the centerman an "offensive genius." Though small at 5-foot-9, Dionne loomed large as the center of the Kings' famed "Triple Crown" line alongside teammates Charlie Simmer and Dave Taylor.

KEN DRYDEN G
Montreal Canadiens (1971–73, 1974–79)

Despite sitting out a season to finish law school, Ken Dryden still managed

Ken Dryden

six Stanley Cups in his eight NHL seasons. The dominant goaltender later wrote a celebrated book, *The Game*, about life in the NHL and became a member of the Canadian parliament.

Games: 397
Wins-Losses-Ties: 258-57-74
Goals against average: 2.24
Save percentage: .922
Shutouts: 46
Stanley Cups: 6
Awards: One Conn Smythe Trophy, one Calder Trophy, five Vezina Trophies

PHIL ESPOSITO c
Chicago Black Hawks (1964–67), Boston Bruins (1967–75), New York Rangers (1975–81)

No player had ever scored 100 points in a season until "Espo" racked up 126 in 1968–69. He used his huge frame to park in front of the opponent's net. That tactic helped Esposito lead the NHL in goals for six straight years from 1969–70 to 1974–75.

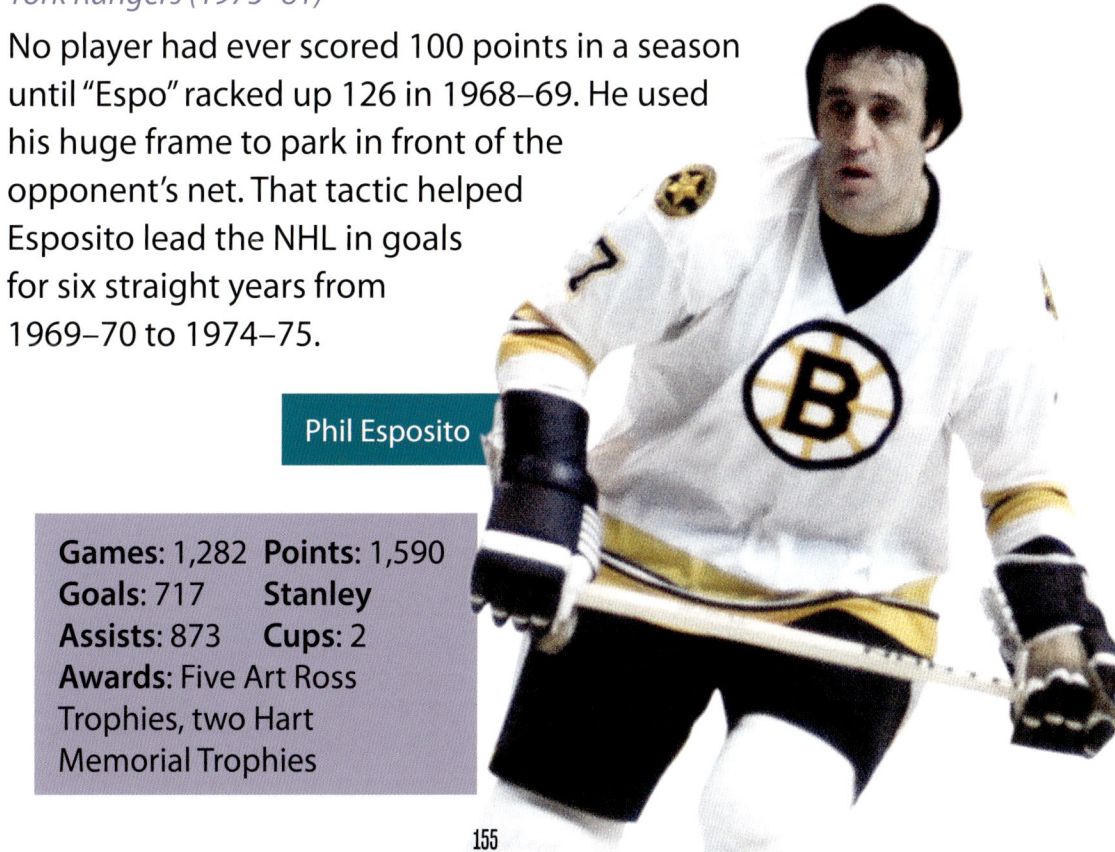

Phil Esposito

Games: 1,282
Goals: 717
Assists: 873
Points: 1,590
Stanley Cups: 2
Awards: Five Art Ross Trophies, two Hart Memorial Trophies

STAR PLAYERS

Tony Esposito

TONY ESPOSITO G
Montreal Canadiens (1968–69), Chicago Black Hawks (1969–84)

Tony Esposito didn't get a lot of playing time for a talented Montreal Canadiens team. But in his first year after joining the Chicago Black Hawks, he posted 15 shutouts. That was the most of any goaltender since the 1920s.

Games: 886
Wins-Losses-Ties: 423–306–152
Goals against average: 2.93
Save percentage: .906
Shutouts: 76
Stanley Cups: 0
Awards: One Calder Trophy, three Vezina Trophies

RON FRANCIS C
Hartford Whalers/Carolina Hurricanes (1981–91, 1998–2004), Pittsburgh Penguins (1991–98), Toronto Maple Leafs (2004)

The quiet Ron Francis was not usually the most recognizable player on his teams. However, by

Ron Francis

the time he retired from the NHL, only Wayne Gretzky had dished out more assists than the player known as "Captain Class."

Games: 1,731 **Points:** 1,798
Goals: 549 **Stanley**
Assists: 1,249 **Cups:** 2
Awards: One Selke Trophy, three Lady Byng Trophies

Mike Gartner

MIKE GARTNER RW

Washington Capitals (1979–89), Minnesota North Stars (1989–90), New York Rangers (1990–94), Toronto Maple Leafs (1994–96), Phoenix Coyotes (1996–98)

An opposing goalie once admitted that he was afraid of Mike Gartner's booming slap shots. The winger used those shots, along with his blazing speed, to score 40 or more goals in nine seasons during his career.

Games: 1,432 **Stanley**
Goals: 708 **Cups:** 0
Assists: 627 **Awards:** None
Points: 1,335

STAR PLAYERS

Bernie Geoffrion

BERNIE GEOFFRION RW
Montreal Canadiens (1950–64), New York Rangers (1966–68)

Bernie "Boom Boom" Geoffrion helped make the slap shot popular during his career. His punishing shots were a big reason goaltenders began to wear masks in the late 1950s and early 1960s.

Games: 883
Goals: 393
Assists: 429
Points: 822
Stanley Cups: 6
Awards: One Calder Trophy, two Art Ross Trophies, one Hart Memorial Trophy

WAYNE GRETZKY C

Edmonton Oilers (1979–88), Los Angeles Kings (1988–96), St. Louis Blues (1996), New York Rangers (1996–99)

Games: 1,487 **Points:** 2,857
Goals: 894 **Stanley**
Assists: 1,963 **Cups:** 4
Awards: Two Conn Smythe Trophies, ten Art Ross Trophies, nine Hart Memorial Trophies, five Lady Byng Trophies

"The Great One" could have played his entire career without scoring a goal and he would still be the NHL's all-time leader in points. His 1,963 assists would be enough on their own. But Wayne Gretzky also retired with a league-record 894 goals. His No. 99 jersey is retired by the entire league as a tribute to his excellence.

Wayne Gretzky

STAR PLAYERS

Glenn Hall

GLENN HALL G
Detroit Red Wings (1952–53, 1955–57), Chicago Black Hawks (1957–67), St. Louis Blues (1967–71)

Glenn Hall backstopped three different teams to the Stanley Cup Final. But he is most famous for starting an NHL-record 502 straight regular-season games in net. What makes the feat even more impressive is that the streak took place before goaltenders wore masks.

Games: 906
Wins-Losses-Ties: 407-326-164
Goals against average: 2.50
Save percentage: .918
Shutouts: 84
Stanley Cups: 1
Awards: One Calder Trophy, one Conn Smythe Trophy, three Vezina Trophies

DOUG HARVEY D
Montreal Canadiens (1947–61), New York Rangers (1961–64), Detroit Red Wings (1967), St. Louis Blues (1967–68)

Before Doug Harvey came along, defensemen generally stayed back and did not join the offense. But Harvey often jumped into the action. Other defensemen came after him and scored

Games: 1,113
Goals: 88
Assists: 452
Points: 540
Stanley Cups: 6
Awards: Seven Norris Trophies

more points, but Harvey changed hockey forever.

DOMINIK HAŠEK G

Chicago Blackhawks (1990–92), Buffalo Sabres (1992–2001), Detroit Red Wings (2001–02, 2003–04, 2006–08), Ottawa Senators (2005–06)

Dominik Hašek might have been the most entertaining goaltender in NHL history. He flailed his body all over the place to stop shots. However, it worked. Hašek led the league in save percentage for six straight seasons in the 1990s and earned the nickname "Dominator."

Dominik Hašek

Doug Harvey

Games: 735
Wins-Losses-Ties/Overtime Losses: 389–223–95
Goals against average: 2.20
Save percentage: .922
Shutouts: 81
Stanley Cups: 2
Awards: Two Hart Memorial Trophies, six Vezina Trophies

STAR PLAYERS

GORDIE HOWE RW
Detroit Red Wings (1946–71), Hartford Whalers (1979–80)

Many people consider Gordie Howe the league's greatest-ever player. Talented, smart, and extremely tough, Howe played professional hockey for 32 years between the NHL and WHA. When he finally retired at age 52, "Mr. Hockey" was playing alongside his two sons, Mark and Marty.

Games: 1,767 **Points:** 1,850
Goals: 801 **Stanley Cups:** 4
Assists: 1,049
Awards: Six Art Ross Trophies, six Hart Trophies

Gordie Howe

BOBBY HULL LW
Chicago Black Hawks (1957–72), Winnipeg Jets (1972–80), Hartford Whalers (1980)

Known as the "Golden Jet" for his speed, showmanship, and flowing blond hair, Bobby Hull was a natural goal scorer. His blistering slap shots powered Hull to more than 600 goals in the NHL. He would have had many more, but he left the NHL for the WHA in the early 1970s.

Games: 1,063
Goals: 610
Assists: 560
Points: 1,170
Stanley Cups: 1
Awards: Three Art Ross Trophies, two Hart Memorial Trophies

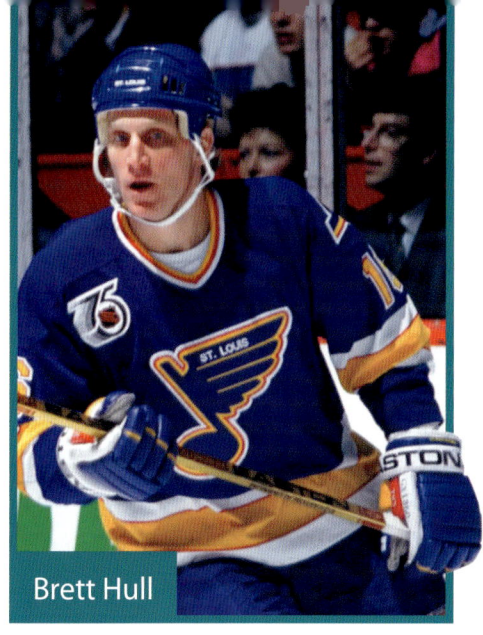

Brett Hull

BRETT HULL RW

Calgary Flames (1986–88), St. Louis Blues (1988–98), Dallas Stars (1998–2001), Detroit Red Wings (2001–04), Phoenix Coyotes (2005)

The son of Bobby Hull, the "Golden Brett" showed that goal scoring runs in the family. Brett Hull scored 86 in 1990–91. Only Wayne Gretzky ever topped that single-season mark.

Games: 1,269 **Points:** 1,391
Goals: 741 **Stanley Cups:** 2
Assists: 650
Awards: One Hart Memorial Trophy, one Lady Byng Trophy

Bobby Hull

STAR PLAYERS

JAROMÍR JÁGR RW

Pittsburgh Penguins (1990–2001), Washington Capitals (2001–04), New York Rangers (2004–08), Philadelphia Flyers (2011–12), Dallas Stars (2012), Boston Bruins (2013), New Jersey Devils (2013–15), Florida Panthers (2015–17), Calgary Flames (2017)

Jaromír Jágr made a splash right away in the early 1990s with his long, curly mullet and offensive skills. He eventually cut his hair, but he never stopped scoring. By the time he left the NHL for good in 2018 he was second on the all-time points list.

Games: 1,733
Points: 1,921
Goals: 766
Assists: 1,155
Stanley Cups: 2
Awards: Five Art Ross Trophies, one Hart Memorial Trophy

Jaromír Jágr

Patrick Kane

PATRICK KANE RW

Chicago Blackhawks (2007–23), New York Rangers (2023), Detroit Red Wings (2023–)

A native of Buffalo, Kane became the first American-born player to win the Art Ross Trophy as the NHL's top scorer in 2015–16. By then he had already led the Chicago Blackhawks to three Stanley Cup victories.

Games: 1,230 **Assists:** 813 **Stanley Cups:** 3
Goals: 471 **Points:** 1,284
Awards: One Art Ross Trophy, one Calder Trophy, one Conn Smythe Trophy, one Hart Memorial Trophy

STAR PLAYERS

Guy Lafleur

GUY LAFLEUR RW

Montreal Canadiens (1971–85), New York Rangers (1988–89), Quebec Nordiques (1989–91)

Games: 1,126
Points: 1,353
Goals: 560
Assists: 793
Stanley Cups: 5
Awards: Three Art Ross Trophies, one Conn Smythe Trophy, three Hart Memorial Trophies

Listed as a right wing, the legendary player known as "the Flower" weaved all over the ice to score at will for the Montreal Canadiens. Guy Lafleur was the first player in NHL history to top 50 goals and 100 points in six straight seasons.

MARIO LEMIEUX C
Pittsburgh Penguins (1984–97, 2000–06)

"Super Mario" took over from Wayne Gretzky as the league's most dominant player in the 1990s. Many fans still wonder if Mario Lemieux could have beaten Gretzky's scoring records. Unfortunately, frequent back injuries and a battle with cancer kept the talented scorer off the ice for long stretches.

Games: 915
Goals: 690
Assists: 1,033
Points: 1,723
Stanley Cups: 2
Awards: One Calder Trophy, five Art Ross Trophies, three Hart Memorial Trophies, two Conn Smythe Trophies

Mario Lemieux

STAR PLAYERS

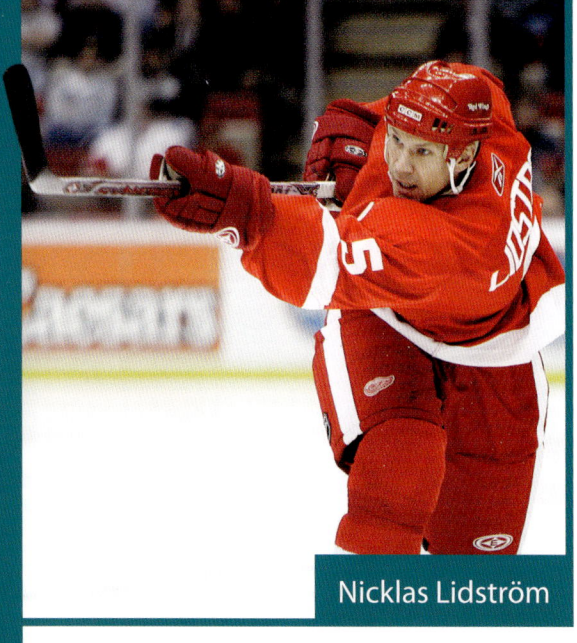

Nicklas Lidström

Games: 1,564	Points: 1,142
Goals: 264	Stanley
Assists: 878	Cups: 4
Awards: One Conn Smythe Trophy, seven Norris Trophies	

NICKLAS LIDSTRÖM D
Detroit Red Wings (1991–2012)

Teammates called Nicklas Lidström the "perfect human." They marveled at the Swedish defenseman's ability to play every night and seemingly never make a mistake. Lidström rarely missed a game as part of the Red Wings dynasty of the 1990s and 2000s.

Ted Lindsay

TED LINDSAY LW
Detroit Red Wings (1944–57, 1964–65), Chicago Black Hawks (1957–60)

"Terrible Ted" was undersized. But he played a physical game alongside linemate Gordie Howe. The well-respected player was honored in 2010 when the Lester B. Pearson Award was renamed the Ted Lindsay Award. The honor is given to the MVP each year as voted on by other NHL players.

Games: 1,068
Goals: 379
Assists: 472
Points: 851
Stanley Cups: 4
Awards: One Art Ross Trophy

CONNOR McDAVID C
Edmonton Oilers (2015–)

Connor McDavid's incredible speed, good vision, and quick hands have made him the face of the NHL in the 2010s and 2020s. In 2022–23, he became the first player to top 150 points in a season since Mario Lemieux did it in 1995–96. That also made him just the sixth player ever to achieve the feat.

Games: 645 **Points:** 982
Goals: 335 **Stanley**
Assists: 647 **Cups:** 0
Awards: Five Art Ross Trophies, three Hart Memorial Trophies

Connor McDavid

Games: 1,756 **Points:** 1,887
Goals: 694   **Stanley**
Assists: 1,193 **Cups:** 6
Awards: One Conn Smythe Trophy, two Hart Memorial Trophies

MARK MESSIER C

Edmonton Oilers (1979–91), New York Rangers (1991–97, 2000–04), Vancouver Canucks (1997–2000)

Mark Messier was known as one of the NHL's most respected leaders. The rugged centerman retired in 2004 as the only player to ever captain two teams to Stanley Cup victories. He won five with the Edmonton Oilers. But he also famously guided the New York Rangers to their first title in 54 years in 1994.

Mark Messier

STAN MIKITA C/RW

Chicago Black Hawks (1958–79)

Stan Mikita set Chicago Blackhawks scoring records. But he also had a lasting legacy in modern hockey equipment. After accidentally bending his flat stick blade in practice one day, Mikita liked the way his curved stick shot the puck. Soon others copied his idea,

Games: 1,396 **Points:** 1,467
Goals: 541   **Stanley**
Assists: 926 **Cups:** 1
Awards: Four Art Ross Trophies, two Hart Memorial Trophies, two Lady Byng Trophies

Stan Mikita

and the curved stick became the standard.

MIKE MODANO C
Minnesota North Stars/Dallas Stars (1989–2010), Detroit Red Wings (2010–11)

Few opponents could slow down Mike Modano when he was flying up the ice at full speed. The Livonia, Michigan, native retired as the all-time leading NHL scorer among US-born players.

Games: 1,499
Goals: 561
Assists: 813
Points: 1,374
Stanley Cups: 1
Awards: None

Mike Modano

STAR PLAYERS

Howie Morenz

HOWIE MORENZ c

Montreal Canadiens (1923–34, 1936–37), Chicago Black Hawks (1934–36), New York Rangers (1936)

Howie Morenz was one of the NHL's earliest superstars. But his career came to a tragic end. Just weeks after a broken leg ended his career at age 34, Morenz died of a coronary embolism. Fifty thousand fans turned up to his funeral, which was held in the Canadiens' home arena.

Games: 550 **Points:** 476
Goals: 271 **Stanley**
Assists: 205 **Cups:** 3
Awards: Three Hart Trophies

BOBBY ORR D

Boston Bruins (1966–75), Chicago Black Hawks (1976–78)

Games: 657 **Points:** 915
Goals: 270 **Stanley Cups:** 2
Assists: 645
Awards: One Calder Trophy, two Art Ross Trophies, three Hart Memorial Trophies, eight Norris Trophies

Though he was a defenseman, Bobby Orr was usually the best offensive player on the ice. He was the first defenseman to ever lead the league in scoring. Orr's eight Norris Trophies are a record, even though he retired at age 30 due to knee problems.

Bobby Orr

STAR PLAYERS

ALEX OVECHKIN LW
Washington Capitals (2005–)

Many thought Wayne Gretzky's record of 894 career goals was unbreakable. But when Alex Ovechkin reached 800 at age 37 he was still going strong. Using his booming shot, the Russian star led the NHL in goals nine times.

Games: 1,426
Goals: 853
Assists: 697
Points: 1,550
Stanley Cups: 1
Awards: One Art Ross Trophy, one Calder Trophy, one Conn Smythe Trophy, three Hart Memorial Trophies

Alex Ovechkin

JACQUES PLANTE G
Montreal Canadiens (1952–63), New York Rangers (1963–64), St. Louis Blues (1968–70), Toronto Maple Leafs (1970–73), Boston Bruins (1973)

Jacques Plante is notable as the first goaltender to regularly mask in a game. But his career was far more than that. The innovative Plante was also one of the first goaltenders to come

Games: 837
Wins-Losses-Ties: 437–246–145
Goals against average: 2.38
Save percentage: .920
Shutouts: 82
Stanley Cups: 6
Awards: One Hart Trophy, seven Vezina Trophies

Jacques Plante

out of the net to cut down shooting angles. He backstopped his hometown Canadiens to five straight Stanley Cups from 1956 to 1960.

DENIS POTVIN D
New York Islanders (1973–88)

Denis Potvin retired after breaking all of Bobby Orr's career scoring records for defensemen. The hard-shooting, hard-hitting Islander was one of the key pieces of New York's four straight Stanley Cup wins between 1979–80 and 1982–83.

Denis Potvin

Games: 1,060
Goals: 310
Assists: 742
Points: 1,052
Stanley Cups: 4
Awards: One Calder Trophy, three Norris Trophies

Games: 1,258
Goals: 358
Assists: 688
Points: 1,046
Stanley Cups: 11
Awards: None

HENRI RICHARD C
Montreal Canadiens (1955–75)

Though Henri Richard was often overshadowed by his older brother Maurice early in his career, his all-around skills made him a star in his own right. Plus, Henri's 11 Stanley Cups are not only the most in the family but the most of any NHL player.

Henri Richard

MAURICE RICHARD RW
Montreal Canadiens (1942–60)

Games: 978 **Points:** 966
Goals: 544 **Stanley**
Assists: 422 **Cups:** 8
Awards: One Hart Trophy

The "Rocket" was a hero to French-speaking Canadian people during and after his career. Maurice Richard was the first player to ever reach 500 NHL goals. Today, the player who scores the most goals in a single season receives the Rocket Richard Trophy.

LARRY ROBINSON D

Montreal Canadiens (1972–89), Los Angeles Kings (1989–92)

Games: 1,384	**Points:** 958
Goals: 208	**Stanley Cups:** 6
Assists: 750	
Awards: One Conn Smythe Trophy, two Norris Trophies	

Nicknamed "Big Bird" after the friendly character from *Sesame Street*, Larry Robinson was anything but nice to opposing forwards. His thumping hits were legendary around the league. Robinson used them to help propel his Canadiens teams to six Stanley Cup victories.

Maurice Richard

Larry Robinson

STAR PLAYERS

Patrick Roy

PATRICK ROY G
Montreal Canadiens (1985–95), Colorado Avalanche (1995–2003)

Few goaltenders were better in big games than Patrick Roy. He was the first player to ever win the Conn Smythe Trophy as playoff MVP three times. He also retired as the all-time leader in regular-season victories.

Games: 1,029
Wins-Losses-Ties: 551–315–131
Goals against average: 2.54
Save percentage: .910
Shutouts: 66
Stanley Cups: 4
Awards: Three Conn Smythe Trophies, three Vezina Trophies

JOE SAKIC C
Quebec Nordiques/Colorado Avalanche (1988–2009)

Joe Sakic never led the league in goals, assists, or points. But when he

Games: 1,378
Goals: 625
Assists: 1,016
Points: 1,641
Stanley Cups: 2
Awards: One Conn Smythe Trophy, one Hart Memorial Trophy, one Lady Byng Trophy

retired he was the NHL's ninth-highest scorer. Sakic was also considered one of the league's best leaders and classiest players.

Joe Sakic

SERGE SAVARD D

Montreal Canadiens (1967–81), Winnipeg Jets (1981–83)

Serge Savard was the leader of Montreal's defense during the team's 1970s dynasty. A crafty, smart player, he was nicknamed *Le Senateur*, or "the Senator." He was a master at breaking up opponents' offensive plays by using his long reach and shot-blocking ability.

Serge Savard

Games: 1,040
Goals: 106
Assists: 333
Points: 439
Stanley Cups: 7
Awards: One Conn Smythe Trophy

STAR PLAYERS

Terry Sawchuk

Games: 971
Wins-Losses-Ties: 445–336–171
Goals against average: 2.50
Save percentage: .907
Shutouts: 103
Stanley Cups: 4
Awards: One Calder Trophy, four Vezina Trophies

TERRY SAWCHUK G

Detroit Red Wings (1950–55, 1957–64, 1968–69), Boston Bruins (1955–57), Toronto Maple Leafs (1964–67), Los Angeles Kings (1967–68), New York Rangers (1969–70)

Terry Sawchuk died at the age of 40 while he was still an active player. At the time of his passing in 1970, he had more wins and shutouts than any goaltender. Both records stood until the 2000s.

TEEMU SELÄNNE RW

Winnipeg Jets (1992–96), Anaheim Ducks (1996–01, 2005–14), San Jose Sharks (2001–03), Colorado Avalanche (2003–04)

Teemu Selänne scored a record 76 goals as a rookie in 1992–93. The "Finnish Flash" never scored that many in a season again. But he managed at least 40 goals six more times.

Games: 1,451
Goals: 684
Assists: 773
Points: 1,457
Stanley Cups: 1
Awards: One Calder Trophy

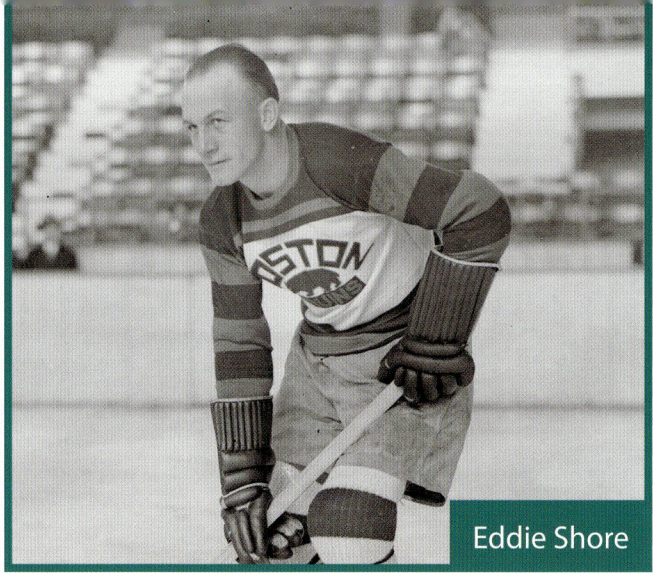

Eddie Shore

Games: 551
Goals: 105
Assists: 179
Points: 284
Stanley Cups: 2
Awards: Four Hart Trophies

EDDIE SHORE D
Boston Bruins (1926–39), New York Americans (1940)

Eddie Shore was an excellent offensive defenseman in his era. But he was best known for his physical play. Shore led the NHL in penalty minutes two times. He once got into so many fights in a game that he spent the night in the hospital.

Teemu Selänne

STAR PLAYERS

Peter Šťastný

PETER ŠŤASTNÝ C
Quebec Nordiques (1980–90), New Jersey Devils (1990–93), St. Louis Blues (1994–95)

Peter Šťastný defected from Czechoslovakia to join the NHL in 1980. That season, he became the first rookie to top 100 points in a season. His success helped convince other Eastern European hockey stars to escape their home countries and head to North America.

Games: 977
Goals: 450
Assists: 789
Awards: One Calder Trophy
Points: 1,239
Stanley Cups: 0

BRYAN TROTTIER C
New York Islanders (1975–90), Pittsburgh Penguins (1990–94)

Bryan Trottier started his career as a gifted scorer. The humble star never lost his offensive skill, but "Trotts" became an

Bryan Trottier

> **Games:** 1,279   **Assists:** 901   **Stanley Cups:** 6
> **Goals:** 524   **Points:** 1,425
> **Awards:** One Art Ross Trophy, one Calder Trophy, one Conn Smythe Trophy, one Hart Memorial Trophy

excellent defensive center and respected leader for six Stanley Cup–winning teams.

STEVE YZERMAN c
Detroit Red Wings (1983–2006)

Steve Yzerman spent an NHL-record 19 seasons as the Red Wings captain between 1986 and 2006. In that time, he helped transform the team from bottom-feeders to an NHL dynasty. The humble Yzerman didn't consider himself a superstar, but he is a legend in Detroit.

> **Games:** 1,514   **Points:** 1,755
> **Goals:** 692   **Stanley Cups:** 3
> **Assists:** 1,063
> **Awards:** One Conn Smythe Trophy, one Selke Trophy

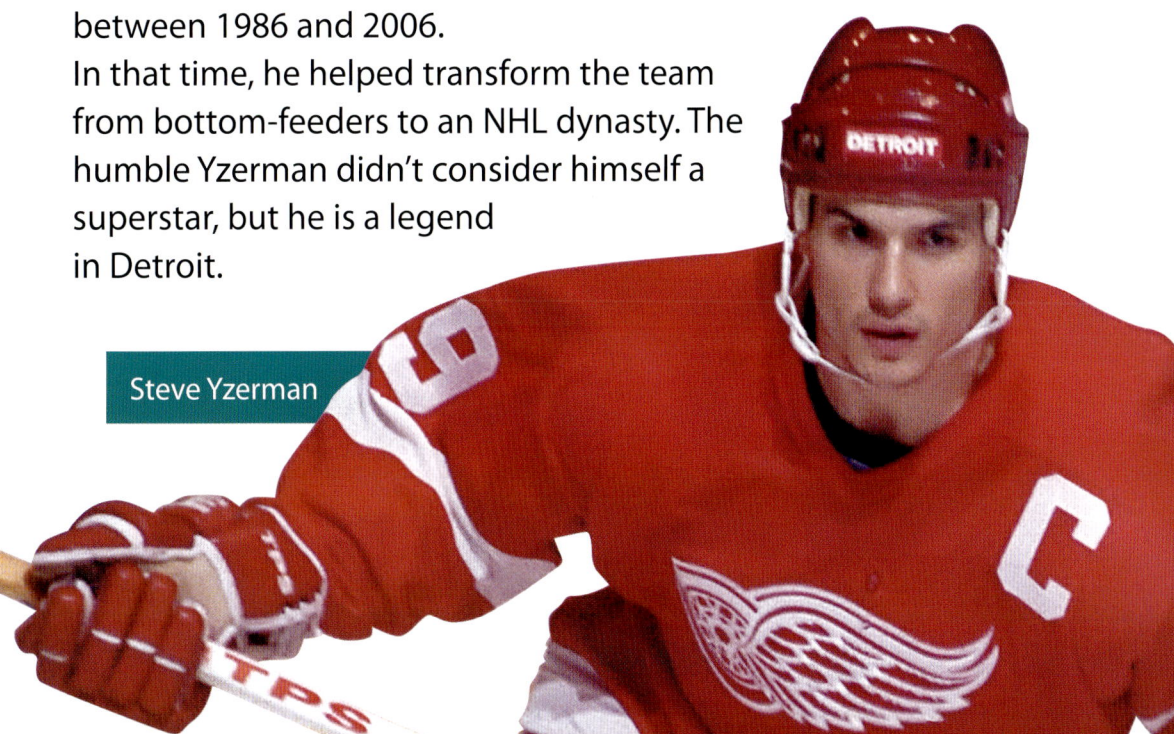

Steve Yzerman

HONORABLE MENTIONS

Sid Abel (C/LW): Detroit Red Wings (1938–43, 1945–52), Chicago Black Hawks (1952–53)

Syl Apps (C): Toronto Maple Leafs (1936–43, 1945–48)

Andy Bathgate (RW): New York Rangers (1952–64), Toronto Maple Leafs (1964–65), Detroit Red Wings (1965–67), Pittsburgh Penguins (1967–68, 1970–71)

Toe Blake (LW): Montreal Maroons (1935), Montreal Canadiens (1935–48)

Turk Broda (G): Toronto Maple Leafs (1936–43, 1945–52)

Johnny Bucyk (LW): Detroit Red Wings (1955–57), Boston Bruins (1957–78)

Pavel Bure (RW): Vancouver Canucks (1991–98), Florida Panthers (1998–2002), New York Rangers (2002–03)

Zdeno Chara (D): New York Islanders (1997–2001, 2021–22), Ottawa Senators (2001–06), Boston Bruins (2006–20), Washington Capitals (2021)

King Clancy (D): Ottawa Senators (1921–30), Toronto Maple Leafs (1930–36)

Bobby Clarke (C): Philadelphia Flyers (1969–84)

Charlie Conacher (RW): Toronto Maple Leafs (1929–38), Detroit Red Wings (1938–39), New York Americans (1939–41)

Yvon Cournoyer (RW): Montreal Canadiens (1963–78)

Alex Delvecchio (C/LW): Detroit Red Wings (1951–73)

Bill Durnan (G): Montreal Canadiens (1943–50)

Sergei Fedorov (C): Detroit Red Wings (1990–2003), Anaheim Ducks (2003–05), Columbus Blue Jackets (2005–08), Washington Capitals (2008–09)

Marc-André Fleury (G): Pittsburgh Penguins (2003–17), Vegas Golden Knights (2017–21), Chicago Blackhawks (2021–22), Minnesota Wild (2022–)

Peter Forsberg (C): Quebec Nordiques/Colorado Avalanche (1994–2004, 2008, 2011), Philadelphia Flyers (2005–07), Nashville Predators (2007)

Grant Fuhr (G): Edmonton Oilers (1981–91), Toronto Maple Leafs (1991–93), Buffalo Sabres (1993–95), Los Angeles Kings (1995), St. Louis Blues (1995–99), Calgary Flames (1999–2000)

Tim Horton (D): Toronto Maple Leafs (1950–70), New York Rangers (1970–71), Pittsburgh Penguins (1971–72), Buffalo Sabres (1972–73)

Jarome Iginla (RW): Calgary Flames (1996–2013), Pittsburgh Penguins (2013), Boston Bruins (2013–14), Colorado Avalanche (2014–17), Los Angeles Kings (2017)

Duncan Keith (D): Chicago Blackhawks (2005–21), Edmonton Oilers (2021–22)

Red Kelly (D/C): Detroit Red Wings (1947–60), Toronto Maple Leafs (1960–67)

Ted Kennedy (C): Toronto Maple Leafs (1943–57)

Dave Keon (C): Toronto Maple Leafs (1960–75), Hartford Whalers (1979–82)

Jari Kurri (RW): Edmonton Oilers (1980–90), Los Angeles Kings (1991–96), New York Rangers (1996), Anaheim Ducks (1996–97), Colorado Avalanche (1997–98)

Elmer Lach (C): Montreal Canadiens (1940–54)

Brian Leetch (D): New York Rangers (1988–2004), Toronto Maple Leafs (2004), Boston Bruins (2005–06)

Al MacInnis (D): Calgary Flames (1981–94), St. Louis Blues (1994–2003)
Frank Mahovlich (LW): Toronto Maple Leafs (1957–68), Detroit Red Wings (1968–71), Montreal Canadiens (1971–74)
Evgeni Malkin (C): Pittsburgh Penguins (2006–)
Dickie Moore (LW): Montreal Canadiens (1951–63), Toronto Maple Leafs (1964–65), St. Louis Blues (1967–68)
Scott Niedermayer (D): New Jersey Devils (1991–2004), Anaheim Ducks (2005–10)
Adam Oates (C): Detroit Red Wings (1985–89), St. Louis Blues (1989–92), Boston Bruins (1992–97), Washington Capitals (1997–2002), Philadelphia Flyers (2002), Anaheim Ducks (2002–03), Edmonton Oilers (2003–04)
Bernie Parent (G): Boston Bruins (1965–67), Philadelphia Flyers (1967–71, 1973–79), Toronto Maple Leafs (1971)
Brad Park (D): New York Rangers (1968–76), Boston Bruins (1976–83), Detroit Red Wings (1983–85)
Gilbert Perreault (C): Buffalo Sabres (1970–86)
Carey Price (G): Montreal Canadiens (2007–22)
Chris Pronger (D): Hartford Whalers (1993–95), St. Louis Blues (1995–2004), Edmonton Oilers (2005–06), Anaheim Ducks (2006–09), Philadelphia Flyers (2009–11)
Jean Ratelle (C): New York Rangers (1961–75), Boston Bruins (1975–81)
Luc Robitaille (LW): Los Angeles Kings (1986–94, 1997–2001, 2003–06), Pittsburgh Penguins (1994–95), New York Rangers (1995–97), Detroit Red Wings (2001–03)
Börje Salming (D): Toronto Maple Leafs (1973–89), Detroit Red Wings (1989–90)
Denis Savard (C): Chicago Blackhawks (1980–90, 1995–97), Montreal Canadiens (1990–93), Tampa Bay Lightning (1993–95)
Milt Schmidt (C/D): Boston Bruins (1936–55)
Brendan Shanahan (LW): New Jersey Devils (1987–91, 2008–09), St. Louis Blues (1991–95), Hartford Whalers (1995–96), Detroit Red Wings (1996–2006), New York Rangers (2006–08)
Darryl Sittler (C): Toronto Maple Leafs (1970–82), Philadelphia Flyers (1982–84), Detroit Red Wings (1984–85)
Scott Stevens (D): Washington Capitals (1982–90), St. Louis Blues (1990–91), New Jersey Devils (1991–2004)
Mats Sundin (C): Quebec Nordiques (1990–94), Toronto Maple Leafs (1994–2008), Vancouver Canucks (2008–09)
Joe Thornton (C): Boston Bruins (1997–2005), San Jose Sharks (2005–20), Toronto Maple Leafs (2020–21), Florida Panthers (2021–22)
Jonathan Toews (C): Chicago Blackhawks (2007–23)
Georges Vezina (G): Montreal Canadiens (1917–25)

NHL ALL-TIME LEADERS (THROUGH 2023–24)

OFFENSIVE LEADERS (REGULAR SEASON)

GAMES PLAYED
1. Patrick Marleau — 1,779
2. Gordie Howe — 1,767
3. Mark Messier — 1,756
4. Jaromír Jágr — 1,733
5. Ron Francis — 1,731

GOALS
1. Wayne Gretzky — 894
2. Alex Ovechkin* — 853
3. Gordie Howe — 801
4. Jaromír Jágr — 766
5. Brett Hull — 741

ASSISTS
1. Wayne Gretzky — 1,963
2. Ron Francis — 1,249
3. Mark Messier — 1,193
4. Ray Bourque — 1,169
5. Jaromír Jágr — 1,155

POINTS
1. Wayne Gretzky — 2,857
2. Jaromír Jágr — 1,921
3. Mark Messier — 1,887
4. Gordie Howe — 1,850
5. Ron Francis — 1,798

HAT TRICKS
1. Wayne Gretzky — 50
2. Mario Lemieux — 40
3. Mike Bossy — 39
4. Brett Hull — 33
5. Phil Esposito — 32

POWER PLAY GOALS
1. Alex Ovechkin* — 312
2. Dave Andreychuk — 274
3. Brett Hull — 265
4. Teemu Selänne — 255
5. Luc Robitaille — 247

SHORTHANDED GOALS
1. Wayne Gretzky — 73
2. Mark Messier — 63
3. Steve Yzerman — 50
4. Mario Lemieux — 49
5. Butch Goring — 39
5. Jari Kurri — 39
5. Dave Poulin — 39

GAME-WINNING GOALS
1. Jaromír Jágr — 135
2. Alex Ovechkin* — 129
3. Gordie Howe — 121
4. Phil Esposito — 118
5. Brett Hull — 110
5. Teemu Selänne — 110

PENALTY MINUTES
1. Tiger Williams — 3,971
2. Dale Hunter — 3,565
3. Tie Domi — 3,515
4. Marty McSorley — 3,381
5. Bob Probert — 3,300

OFFENSIVE LEADERS (PLAYOFFS)

GAMES PLAYED
1. Chris Chelios — 266
2. Nicklas Lidström — 263
3. Mark Messier — 236
4. Claude Lemieux — 234
5. Scott Stevens — 233

GOALS
1. Wayne Gretzky — 122
2. Mark Messier — 109
3. Jari Kurri — 106
4. Brett Hull — 103
5. Glenn Anderson — 93

ASSISTS
1. Wayne Gretzky — 260
2. Mark Messier — 186
3. Ray Bourque — 139
4. Paul Coffey — 137
5. Sidney Crosby* — 130

POINTS
1. Wayne Gretzky — 382
2. Mark Messier — 295
3. Jari Kurri — 233
4. Glenn Anderson — 214
5. Jaromír Jágr — 201
5. Sidney Crosby* — 201

HAT TRICKS
1. Wayne Gretzky — 10
2. Maurice Richard — 7
2. Jari Kurri — 7
4. Dino Ciccarelli — 6
5. Mike Bossy — 5

POWER PLAY GOALS
1. Brett Hull — 38
2. Mike Bossy — 35
2. Wayne Gretzky — 35
4. Dino Ciccarelli — 34
5. Nicklas Lidström — 30
5. Joe Pavelski — 30

SHORTHANDED GOALS
1. Mark Messier _____ 14
2. Wayne Gretzky _____ 12
3. Jari Kurri _____ 10
4. Ed Westfall _____ 8
4. Håkan Loob _____ 8

GAME-WINNING GOALS
1. Wayne Gretzky _____ 24
1. Brett Hull _____ 24
3. Claude Lemieux _____ 19
3. Joe Sakic _____ 19
5. Maurice Richard _____ 18
5. Joe Pavelski _____ 18

GOALTENDING LEADERS (REGULAR SEASON)

GAMES PLAYED
1. Martin Brodeur _____ 1,266
2. Roberto Luongo _____ 1,044
3. Patrick Roy _____ 1,029
4. Marc-André Fleury* _____ 1,025
5. Terry Sawchuk _____ 971

GOALS AGAINST AVERAGE
1. Alec Connell _____ 1.92
2. George Hainsworth _____ 1.93
3. Charlie Gardiner _____ 2.02
4. Lorne Chabot _____ 2.03
5. Tiny Thompson _____ 2.07

SHUTOUTS
1. Martin Brodeur _____ 125
2. Terry Sawchuk _____ 103
3. George Hainsworth _____ 94
4. Glenn Hall _____ 84
5. Jacques Plante _____ 82

WINS
1. Martin Brodeur _____ 691
2. Marc-André Fleury* _____ 561
3. Patrick Roy _____ 551
4. Roberto Luongo _____ 489
5. Ed Belfour _____ 484

SAVE PERCENTAGE
1. Dominik Hašek _____ .9223
2. Johnny Bower _____ .9219
3. Ken Dryden _____ .9215
4. Tuukka Rask _____ .9210
5. Ben Bishop _____ .9205

GOALTENDING LEADERS (PLAYOFFS)

GAMES PLAYED
1. Patrick Roy _____ 247
2. Martin Brodeur _____ 205
3. Marc-André Fleury* ____ 169
4. Ed Belfour _____ 161
5. Grant Fuhr _____ 150

GOALS AGAINST AVERAGE
(MIN. 25 GAMES)
1. Flat Walsh _____ .74
2. Thatcher Demko* _____ .97
3. Joe Miller _____ 1.00
4. Kevin Poulin* _____ 1.14
5. Chad Johnson _____ 1.16

SHUTOUTS
1. Martin Brodeur _____ 24
2. Patrick Roy _____ 23
3. Curtis Joseph _____ 16
3. Marc-André Fleury* _ 16
5. Chris Osgood _____ 15

*indicates player is active as of 2024

WINS
1. Patrick Roy _____ 151
2. Martin Brodeur _____ 113
3. Grant Fuhr _____ 92
3. Marc-André Fleury* _ 92
5. Billy Smith _____ 88
5. Ed Belfour _____ 88

SAVE PERCENTAGE
(MIN. 25 GAMES)
1. Tim Thomas _____ .933
2. Jonas Hiller _____ .930
3. Craig Anderson* ___ .929
4. Igor Shesterkin* __ .9276
5. Olaf Kölzig _____ .9273

GLOSSARY

bankrupt
Unable to pay debts.

contender
A team that has a good chance to win championships.

coronary embolism
A blood clot in a person's heart that causes an artery to be blocked.

defect
To leave one's country permanently, often for political reasons.

deke
A move in which a player fakes a motion to fool an opposing player.

dynasty
An extended period of excellence or success for a team.

expansion
The addition of new teams to increase the size of a league.

fold
To go out of business.

franchise
A professional sports team that is part of a league.

lockout
When management prevents employees from reporting to work.

merge
To combine two or more organizations to create a single larger one.

negotiation
The process of coming to formal agreements.

province
One of the regional divisions of Canada.

restrict
To prevent from doing something.

rookie
An athlete in his or her first full season in a sport.

seed
A rank assigned to a player or a team in a tournament.

upset
To unexpectedly beat a team that was heavily favored to win.

TO LEARN MORE

FURTHER READINGS

Clarke, David J. *Hockey Strategies*. Abdo, 2024.

Hewson, Anthony K. *GOATs of Hockey*. Abdo, 2022.

Zweig, Eric. *Hockey Hall of Fame True Stories*. Firefly, 2022.

ONLINE RESOURCES

To learn more about the NHL, please visit **abdobooklinks.com** or scan this QR code. These links are routinely monitored and updated to provide the most current information available.

INDEX

Arnott, Jason, 87

Bedard, Connor, 41
Béliveau, Jean, 77–78, 148, 150
Binnington, Jordan, 118–119
Bossy, Mike, 89–90, 148
Bourque, Ray, 25–26, 47, 149
Bower, Johnny, 125, 150
Brodeur, Martin, 85–86, 150

Chelios, Chris, 41–42, 151
Coffey, Paul, 60–61, 152
COVID-19 pandemic, 122
Crosby, Sidney, 17, 104–107, 152

Datsyuk, Pavel, 57, 153
Dionne, Marcel, 69–70, 154
draft, 28, 41, 47, 56, 135, 140
Dryden, Ken, 77–78, 154–155

Esposito, Phil, 24–26, 155
Esposito, Tony, 41–42, 156

Fleury, Marc-André, 105–107, 137–138
Francis, Ron, 37–38, 105, 156–157

Gartner, Mike, 141, 157
Geoffrion, Bernie, 77, 158
Giguère, Jean-Sébastien, 21, 23
Gretzky, Wayne, 13–14, 60–62, 68–69, 85, 152, 157, 159, 163, 167, 174

Hall of Fame, 44, 47, 78
Hall, Glenn, 41, 43, 58, 160
Harvey, Doug, 77, 160–161
Hašek, Dominik, 29–30, 161

Howe, Gordie, 7, 56–58, 162, 168
Hull, Bobby, 41–43, 162
Hull, Brett, 55, 117–118, 163

Jágr, Jaromír, 104–105, 164

Kane, Patrick, 41, 43, 165
Krupp, Uwe, 47

Lafleur, Guy, 77–78, 166
Lemieux, Mario, 104–106, 167, 169
Lidström, Nicklas, 57, 107, 168
Lindros, Eric, 47, 101
Lindsay, Ted, 56–57, 143, 168–169
Lorentz, Jim, 31

MacInnis, Al, 33–35, 117
MacLeish, Rick, 101, 103
Martinez, Alec, 71
Masterton, Bill, 55
McDavid, Connor, 61, 169
McDonald, Lanny, 33
Messier, Mark, 60–61, 93–94, 170
Mikita, Stan, 41–43, 170–171
Modano, Mike, 53–54, 171
Morenz, Howie, 77, 172

National Hockey Association (NHA), 4
Nystrom, Bob, 89–90

Original Six, 6–8, 11, 59, 92, 116, 124
Orr, Bobby, 11, 24–25, 27, 173, 175
Otto, Joel, 35
Ovechkin, Alex, 17, 140–143, 174

Perreault, Gilbert, 28–30
Plante, Jacques, 77, 126, 174–175
Potvin, Denis, 89, 175

Rhéaume, Manon, 121
Richard, Henri, 77–78, 176
Richard, Maurice, 7, 77–78, 176
Robinson, Larry, 77, 177
Roy, Patrick, 45–46, 178

Sakic, Joe, 45–47, 178–179
Savard, Serge, 77, 179
Sawchuk, Terry, 57–59, 180
Sedin, Daniel, 133–135
Sedin, Henrik, 133–135
Selänne, Teemu, 21–22, 180
Shore, Eddie, 25, 181
Stanley Cup history, 5
Šťastný, Peter, 45–46, 182
Stone, Mark, 136–137, 139

Toews, Jonathan, 41
Trottier, Bryan, 89–90, 182

Vasilevskiy, Andrei, 121–123

Ward, Cam, 37–39
Ward, Joel, 111
World Hockey Association (WHA), 11, 13, 36, 44, 60, 88, 128, 162

Yzerman, Steve, 56–58, 183

PHOTO CREDITS

Cover Photos: Steve Babineau/National Hockey League/Getty Images, front (Patrick Roy); G. Fiume/Getty Images Sport/Getty Images, front (Alex Ovechkin); Robert Shaver/Bruce Bennett Collection/Getty Images, front (Mario Lemeiux); Claus Andersen/Getty Images Sport/Getty Images, front (Matthew Tkacuk); Ethan Miller/Getty Images Sport/Getty Images, front (Connor Bedard); Andy Devlin/National Hockey League/Getty Images, front (Connor McDavid); B. Bennett/Bruce Bennett Studios/Getty Images, front (Wayne Gretzky); J. D. Cuban/Getty Images Sport/Getty Images, back (Mighty Ducks Mascot); Bruce Bennett/Getty Images Sport/Getty Images, back (Sidney Crosby)

Interior Photos: Matthew Stockman/Getty Images, 1, 169; Steve Babineau/National Hockey League/Getty Images, 3; Bruce Bennett Studios/Getty Images Studios/Getty Images, 4, 8, 9, 10, 12, 31, 35, 48, 68, 77, 88, 124, 125, 149 (top), 154 (top), 157, 159, 168 (bottom), 176, 177 (right), 180; AP Images, 6, 56, 76, 148, 158, 172, 173, 175 (top); UPI/Bettmann Archive/Getty Images, 7; Bruce Bennett Studios/Getty Images/Getty Images, 13; Bruce Bennett/Bruce Bennett Studios/Getty Images, 14, 160, 166, 167, 175 (bottom); Brian Bahr/Getty Images, 16; Chris Tanouye/Freestyle Photography/Getty Images, 17; Harry How/Getty Images, 18, 23, 135, 137, 147; Eliot J. Schechter/NHLI/Getty Images, 19; Mark J. Terrill/AP Images, 20; Paul Sakuma/AP Images, 22; Yoon S. Byun/The Boston Globe/Getty Images, 24; IHA/Icon SMI/Icon Sportswire, 25; Ray Lussier/Boston Herald American/AP Images, 27; Robert Shaver/Bruce Bennett Collection/Bruce Bennett Studios/Getty Images, 28, 32, 36, 154 (bottom); Doug Pensinger/ALLSPORT/Getty Images, 29; Graig Abel/Getty Images, 34, 52, 53, 84, 117, 127, 128, 132, 149 (bottom), 151, 152, 156 (top), 156 (bottom), 182 (bottom), 183; Jim McIsaac/Getty Images, 37, 99, 144; Jaylynn Nash/Getty Images, 39; Bettmann/Getty Images, 40, 42, 177 (left), 181 (top); Kathy Willens/AP Images, 43; Jared Silber/NHLI/Getty Images, 44; Doug Pensinger/Getty Images, 45; Bruce Bennett/Getty Images, 46, 59, 60, 63, 86, 92, 100, 101, 103, 107, 116, 138, 143; Kirk Irwin/Getty Images, 49, 51; Gene Puskar/AP Images, 55; Tom Pidgeon/AP Images, 58; Alex Gallardo/AP Images, 61; Rick Stewart/Allsport/Getty Images Sport/Getty Images, 64; Rich Storry/Getty Images, 66; Peter Joneleit/Icon Sportswire/Getty Images, 67; Dave Buston/AP Images, 69; Bob Frid/Icon Sportswire, 71; Andy King/AP Images, 72; Frederick Breedon/Getty Images, 73; Bruce Bennett Studios/Getty Images, 75; Focus on Sport/Getty Images, 79, 179 (bottom); Harry How/Allsport/Getty Images, 80; Dilip Vishwanat/Getty Images, 83 (top), 119; Mark Humphrey/AP Images, 83 (bottom); Bill Kostroun/AP Images, 87, 150 (bottom); Minas Panagiotakis/Getty Images, 89; Richard Drew/AP Images, 91; Ron Frehm/AP Images, 93, 170; Kostas Lymperopoulos/Cal Sport Media/AP Images, 95; Rick Stewart/Getty Images Sport/Getty Images, 96; Harry How/NHLI/Getty Images Sport/Getty Images, 97; Melchior DiGiacomo/Getty Images, 104; Gene J. Puskar/AP Images, 105, 153 (bottom), 164; Ian Tomlinson/Allsport/Getty Images, 108; Chris Carlson/AP Images, 110; Rocky W. Widner/NHL/Getty Images, 111; Karen Ducey/Getty Images, 112; Steph Chambers/Getty Images, 113; Christopher Mast/NHLI/Getty Images, 115; Mike Carlson/AP Images, 120; David Zalubowski/AP Images, 123 (top), 178; LM Otero/AP Images, 123 (bottom); Jonathan Daniel/Getty Images, 129; Chris Gardner/Getty Images, 131; Jeff Vinnick/Getty Images, 133; Ethan Miller/Getty Images, 136, 139; Graig Abel Collection/Getty Images, 140; Luis M. Alvarez/AP Images, 141; Jonathan Kozub/NHLI/Getty Images, 145; Pictorial Parade/Hulton Archive/Getty Images, 150 (top); Tom Pidgeon/NHLI/Getty Images, 153 (top); Steve Babineau/NHLI/Getty Images, 155, 161 (top); Pictorial Parade/Getty Images, 161 (bottom); Denis Brodeur/NHLI/Getty Images, 162, 163 (top), 163 (bottom), 181 (bottom); Michael Reaves/Getty Images, 165; Paul Sancya/AP Images, 168 (top); Edward Kitch/AP Images, 171 (top); Steve Crandall/Getty Images, 171 (bottom); Keith Srakocic/AP Images, 174; Robert Laberge/Allsport/Getty Images, 179 (top); Scott Levy/Getty Images, 182 (top); Dusty Cline/Shutterstock Images, 185; Alexandr Grant/Shutterstock Images, 187

ABDOBOOKS.COM

Published by Abdo Reference, a division of ABDO, PO Box 398166, Minneapolis, Minnesota 55439. Copyright © 2025 by Abdo Consulting Group, Inc. International copyrights reserved in all countries. No part of this book may be reproduced in any form without written permission from the publisher. Encyclopedias™ is a trademark and logo of Abdo Reference.

Printed in China.
102024
012025

Editor: Arnold Ringstad
Series Designer: Colleen McLaren
Production Designer: Laura Kuchar

LIBRARY OF CONGRESS CONTROL NUMBER: 2024938490

PUBLISHER'S CATALOGING-IN-PUBLICATION DATA

Names: Clarke, David J., author.
Title: The NHL encyclopedia / by David J. Clarke
Description: Minneapolis, Minnesota: Abdo Reference, 2025 | Series: Sports encyclopedias | Includes online resources and index.
Identifiers: ISBN 9781098296094 (lib. bdg.) | ISBN 9798384917090 (eBook)
Subjects: LCSH: National Hockey League--Juvenile literature. | Professional sports--Juvenile literature. | Athletics--Juvenile literature. | Ice hockey--Juvenile literature. | Sports--History--Juvenile literature.
Classification: DDC 796.9626--dc23